EVERYTHING
YOU WANT TO KNOW
ABOUT THE
BIBLE

EVERYTHING
YOU WANT TO KNOW
ABOUT THE
BIBLE

WELL...MAYBE NOT
EVERYTHING
BUT ENOUGH TO
GET YOU STARTED

PETER DOWNEY & BEN SHAW

ZONDERVAN™

GRAND RAPIDS, MICHIGAN 49530 USA

ZONDERVAN™

Everything You Want to Know about the Bible
Copyright © 2005 by OZDAD, a division of Sons of Thunder Press
Originally titled *Inspired Stuff: Everything You Wanted to Know about the Bible but Were Afraid to Ask*
First published in Australia in 2004 by Sons of Thunder Press
First edition: Edited by Mamie Long and designed by firingminds.com

Requests for information should be addressed to:

Zondervan, *Grand Rapids, Michigan 49530*

Library of Congress Cataloging-in-Publication Data

Downey, Peter, 1964–
    Everything you want to know about the bible : well—maybe not everything but
enough to get you started / Peter Downey and Ben Shaw.
       p. cm.
    ISBN-10: 0-310-26504-5 (pbk.)
    ISBN-13: 978-0-310-26504-7 (pbk.)
    1. Bible—Introductions.   I. Shaw, Ben (Ben James), 1968–   II. Title.
    BS475.3.D68 2005
    220.6'1—dc22
                                             2005011497

Interior design by Tracey Walker

Printed in the United States of America

---

05 06 07 08 09 10 11 12 /❖ DCI/ 10 9 8 7 6 5 4 3 2 1

The best book to read is the Bible.
The best book to read is the Bible.
If you read it every day,
It will help you on your way.
The best book to read is the Bible.

– Traditional

CONTENTS

Part 2
THE BIG PICTURE

The Old Testament

The New Testament

STUFF AT THE BACK

STUFF AT THE FRONT

Every word in this foreword keeps you from the fantastic material you are about to read. So I'll be brief.

My first encounter with the Bible did not come through Sunday school, church services or family devotions. (If your background is anything like mine, you'll be wondering what on earth "family devotions" are.) My first experience with the Bible came through a volunteer Scripture teacher. I was sixteen years old, and believe me, religion was the last thing on my mind. Yet somehow this middle-aged mum, with her quick wit and obvious passion for things spiritual, was able to captivate my smart-aleck attention. She knew full well that most in her class were only there because the alternative was the "Non-Scripture" class, which involved the supervision of a real teacher, one who could actually get you into trouble. She didn't seem to mind, though. She was unnervingly content to talk about her beloved Bible to the wildest, most disinterested students.

One day she went a step further and invited the whole class to her home, which was just down the road from school, for Friday afternoon Bible studies. Yeah right! Who would give up their Friday afternoons just to learn about the Bible? Not me. So I went for other reasons: she promised never-ending hamburgers, milkshakes and scones. Only now do I realise how unfair that was. What sixteen-year-old boy can resist the offer of unlimited food?

So one Friday I turned up at her home with five or six friends – Ben Shaw among them – ate her food and braced myself for the inevitable "Bible-bashing". Actually, she already had us completely beaten. She could have been a witch plotting to turn us into newts and there would have been nothing we could have done. We ate so much food, I remember thinking, "I can't get up out of the couch." Then, at that exact moment, she brought out the Bible. There was nowhere to run. So instead, I listened, asked questions and thought hard – things that did not come naturally. There was something about that book and its central character that began to get under my skin.

I went back the following Friday afternoon, the one after that and the one after that. I went back for Bible-and-scone sessions for the next two years. Something had happened. That book I'd never owned, let alone read, was now … well … alive, speaking to me as if we were old friends. It knew me and my world. It made promises to me. It had begun to change me. That was a long time ago, but still, after a couple of degrees in theology and biblical history and more than a decade of writing about and teaching the Bible, I find myself fascinated, daunted and thrilled by this "living" book: even more so after reading *Everything You Want to Know about the Bible*.

Admittedly, my motives for writing this foreword are not entirely pure. First, I am eager to get my name associated with such a great book. Having read Ben and Pete's work, I am very disappointed it's not my book. I'll have to settle for writing this small part. Second, Ben and Pete are mates, and what are mates for if you can't write in each other's books! Maybe after these guys are rich and famous, they'll write forewords for my books. Third – and here's the only reason that counts – *Everything You Want to Know about the Bible* is a first-rate introduction to and overview and exposé of God's Word, the Bible. Pete and Ben have done an enormous service to believers and spectators alike: they have taken complex historical and theological issues surrounding the Bible and told them like a great yarn; they have taken the soaring, life-changing message of the Bible and faithfully re-presented it in a digestible, yet faithful, bite-size form. No matter who you are – new or old Christian, atheist, Bible study leader, theology student, Scripture teacher or minister – you will benefit from this book, especially since by the end of it, I'm sure you'll find yourself reaching for that other book, wanting to plumb its depths for yourself.

So, with a mixture of jealousy (that I didn't write this book first) and excitement (knowing what you are about to read), I hand you over to Ben and Pete.

– Rev. Dr. John Dickson
Sydney, Australia

I f you're going to read a book like this, it's important to know a bit about the authors, B. J. Shaw and P. D. Downey, a.k.a. Ben and Pete.

A book is a reflection of the authors' upbringing, education, experience and beliefs. So you may be more inclined to trust us as authors of a book about the Bible if you know that we are both married and live in red brick houses in the suburbs, as opposed to Raleans who recently returned from an interesting alien-spaceship kidnapping experience.

The important thing is we are both Christian blokes* – as in real, practising Christians, not just "what we say in the census" Christians.

We are both in our thirties, were raised on the northern beaches of Sydney, Australia, and have been Christians for about twenty years. Theologically, we come from a gospel-centred evangelical tradition, which means we believe Jesus is "the way, the truth and the life" and the Bible is the inspired Word of God and all Christians should learn to play the twelve-string guitar so they can force little kids to sing "God said to Noah there's gonna be a floody-floody . . ."

Ben

. . . was born in Vancouver, Canada, but moved to Australia several years later. He grew up in Sydney and spent every spare moment playing sport. During high school, he and a few mates* became Christians through contact with their Scripture teacher, and they began telling their friends about their new faith. In 1984, while still in school, he and three other mates formed a rock band called In the Silence and began touring extensively throughout Australia and New Zealand playing and speak-

ing at music festivals, pubs, schools, universities and prisons. They released several CDs, and their music took them to Holland, England and the USA.

Ben went on to study theology but continued to travel and perform musically with John Dickson, lead singer from the band. After completing his theological degree, Ben began working as assistant minister in Roseville, Australia, where he started a Master's in Ancient History. He now works at a church in Wimbledon, UK.

*Aussie talk for "friend".

For relaxation, Ben plays competitive cricket and soccer and enjoys dinners with friends with the occasional pint of Guinness. His greatest love is his wife, Karen.

Pete

. . . at various times has been a youth leader, Sunday school supervisor, beach mission leader, Christian studies teacher, preacher, Bible study leader and service station attendant, although pumping gas didn't help him write this book. He played and toured in a Christian rock band called Priority Paid for ten years, releasing some CDs and soaring to new heights of anonymity.

On the home front, Pete is married and has three daughters, whom he loves and adores, except when they won't do their piano practise. He has an eight-seater van and a cherry-red left-handed Maton guitar. While Pete has a penchant for the easy reading style of both New Living Translation and Today's New International Version, his Bible of choice remains the NIV Study Bible, because aside from being informative, it weighs several kilograms, making it invaluable in potential self-defence situations.

Holding bachelor, master's and doctorate degrees, his academic background is in education as a teacher of high school English. Although he holds a diploma in biblical studies, he feels like a guy writing a book about automotive engineering when all he's done is worked part-time in a car wash.

Pete has published three internationally best-selling books on marriage and parenting, a book about Jesus for the Bible Society and articles for a range of journals and publications.

*I am normal and Ben is vague.   —Pete

Inspired with confidence?

Good. All you need to know is that we are vaguely normal Christian guys* with a passion for the Bible. We both think it is the most awesome, life-changing, interesting, informative, confronting and exciting book anyone could ever read. And neither of us wear socks under our sandals.

ABOUT THIS BOOK

This is a book about the Bible. The Bible is an important book – no, it is *the* important book. If you ever end up going to a desert island and can only take one book, well, the Bible is the one, although *The Island Castaway Survival Manual* would obviously be a significant temptation.

The Bible sits in a literary category by itself above and beyond all other books. In the bookshelves of the world, it is the top of the heap, the burger with the lot, the best-seller of best-sellers, the top dog, the king of the library, the el supremo.

As the central book of the Christian faith, the Bible is to the Christian what a manufacturer's manual is to a car fanatic. It is the guidebook and the single most important source of information, inspiration, wisdom, encouragement, teaching, advice and fuel consumption that a Christian can get.

The Bible is God's word to us. In it, we read about who God is, what he's done in the world and how we can be in relationship with him. It tells us things about God that otherwise we could not know, and without it we would never know him. It is a book that gives us exciting and unique information about God, history, the world and ourselves.

It all revolves around the central character and the central event of history, when the Son of God, Jesus, lived among us on this earth. It's all about his life, his work, his teachings, his death at the hands of the Roman government and his coming back from death and appearing to people a few days later. It is because of Jesus that we can get right with God and be in relationship with him forever. This is pretty good stuff (the very reason one of the translations of the Bible is called *Good News!*).

Sure, *How to Win Friends and Influence People* can teach you to use someone's name so they'll be really impressed. *Chicken Soup for the Soul* can tell you warm, fuzzy stories that give you soft, squishy feelings. *The Seven Habits of Highly Effective People* can teach you how to think win-win. And *How to Be More Interesting* can teach you ... well, um ... say, did you hear the one about the goldfish and the ... oh, never mind. But while these guidebooks to life might help you through a business meeting, first date or emotional crisis, they're all second-rate, pale imitations to the ultimate "manufacturer's manual". Yep, the Bible is an important book. However, it is often misunderstood.

Case in point: one day recently Ben got into a discussion with a bloke who thought the Bible was just an enormous collection of moralistic lists of

> The Bible is the guidebook and the single most important source of information, inspiration, wisdom, encouragement, teaching, advice and fuel consumption that a Christian can get.

hard-to-keep rules (like Don't drink, Don't swear and Don't be jealous of your neighbour's donkey, or something like that) interspersed with a bunch of stupid kids' stories about giants, whales, floods and blind people getting their sight back.

It was immediately clear that this guy had absolutely no idea what he was talking about. But that was only because he'd obviously not looked at the Bible since he was eight years old.

Many people have an opinion about the Bible, whether they've read it or not; it's usually a patchwork knowledge, an amalgam of ideas and random verses they've picked up over the years: in Scripture classes they've coloured in a work sheet about a guy who got a really good coat and became mates with Pharaoh; they went to a wedding and heard how love is patient and kind; at an uncle's funeral there was something about dust to dust; they saw the Dreamworks cartoon Prince of Egypt; they know that song with the catchy chorus "Turn, turn, turn", which apparently is from the Old Testament somewhere; and to top it off, at an Italian restaurant once for dessert they had an apple gelato dipped in white chocolate, called "Adam's Temptation". They slap these bits together into a cocktail of misconceptions, and *Whammo!* they're a Bible expert.

This is like picking up the *Complete Works of William Shakespeare* and reading ten paragraphs from random pages. Your understanding would be sketchy, to say the least. Many people perceive the Bible as being an ancient and irrelevant book; a mystical and impossible-to-decipher book; a quaint historical book written by ignorant, primitive people who didn't even have cable television; a mysterious and antiquated book of wise sayings and improbable tales that you can let fall open anywhere and your eyes will immediately fall upon a sweet bit of inspiration to get you through the day. To these people, the Bible is an unknown quantity, an unfathomable book outside their experience and beyond their comprehension.

But you don't want to be like that, do you? Of course not! And that's exactly why we wrote this book.

This book is a modest (and somewhat presumptuous) attempt to:

1. **Tell you all about the Bible**
2. **Give you some useful background information**
3. **Summarize what you'll find between its covers**
4. **Encourage and help you to read it**

Of course, it's one thing to have lofty aspirations. It's another to put them into practise. So here's how we've tried to do it. This book has two main parts:

Part 1: The Great Journey provides background information about the Bible. Where did it come from, who wrote it, when was it written, what's it all about,

> Yep, the Bible is an important book. However, it is often misunderstood.

how did it make it to the twenty-first century and is it true that catfish have over 27,000 taste buds?*

Part 2: The Big Picture delves into the content of the Bible itself. But with a book as immense and complex as the Bible, one of the first questions we had to answer was, how do we go about presenting it in a simple way?

We thought about doing a chapter for each book of the Bible, but this was too bitsy. (Imagine cutting an apple pie into sixty-six slices.) Next, we thought about breaking up the narrative into hundred-year units, but there are so many reasons why this was a stupid idea that we won't even begin to list them, and Pete is sorry he ever mentioned it in the first place. Next, we contemplated doing it by literary type, like History, Wisdom, Prophecy, Gospel, Epistle . . . After a long period of negotiation (which involved Ben beating Pete in an arm wrestle), we decided to create a map of the Bible to take you through the significant periods, events and key people.

Before we go on, though, there are three things to get straight.

First, this book is a general overview that moves through the Bible at great speed. It is an introduction to the wonderful richness, depth and diversity of the Bible, its people, its time and its history. This is not an academic tome. Some things dealt with here in passing are the topic of a hundred-thousand-word doctoral thesis or a book so big you could use it to jack up your car to change a tyre. Controversial issues, theological debates, curious asides, fascinating historiographical anecdotes, technical aspects and detailed explanations have been deftly hurdled, because otherwise this book would be the size of a set of encyclopaedias. We really only scratch the surface of the amazing Bible and its theology, linguistics, geography, history and people.

The Bible is incredibly complex, and we are the first to admit that our humble book is a snack-food treatment rather than a gourmet feast. In fact, in writing this book, we're more aware now of our inadequacies as biblical scholars than when we first started out. The more you know about the Bible, the more you know there is *more* to know about the Bible.

However, we reckon this book is a pretty decent springboard from which to dive into the pool of the Bible and swim a few laps. So if you're new to the Bible, or if your knowledge needs a spit and polish, if you think Habakkuk is an infectious disease, or you just want some general reading, then this book is probably your speed. If you're a theology student, however, writing an essay on the use of Hebrew verbs in the prophetic literature of the Old Testament, you should be ashamed of yourself. Go do some real reading.

Second, keep in mind that this book is merely an introduction to the Bible and under no circumstances is it to be used as a replacement for the Bible itself. If you have ever travelled overseas, you've probably bought a guidebook to help you get around. These guidebooks are very informative and helpful,

> The more you know about the Bible, the more you know there is *more* to know about the Bible.

often containing vital information and photos, as well as important phrases like "Where are the pastries?" and "Your mother-in-law is very beautiful."

However, you'd never sit at home and read a guidebook for fun. Its only value lies in the fact that it sheds light on foreign towns, helps you explore the streets and pastry shops and allows you to get on well with any mothers-in-law you may happen to meet. The same applies to this book. Hopefully it will help you explore the pages of the Bible with greater confidence and knowledge. It is not a book to be read as an end in itself. Our aim is to give you the big picture about what the Bible is, when it was written, who wrote it, how it came together and what it's got to say. We hope you'll be able to read the Bible with greater clarity, confidence and understanding and let the words have an impact on your life.*

And hopefully, you will come to understand that the Bible is not some whacky, mystical, ancient and irrelevant volume but the most fascinating, entertaining and life-changing book you'll ever read. Its stories of grace, forgiveness, pain, love and salvation are enthralling. Its words of wisdom, powerful. Its teachings, awesome. Its people, inspiring. Its action, exciting. Its message, challenging. And what it tells you about its main topic – Jesus – will change your life. It is no underestimation to say, quite simply, that there is nothing else like it.

It is an important book that is just as relevant today as it was when the original writers first put their fingers to the keyboard – or if you want to be picky, put their writing sticks to stretched calfskins.

A word of warning: Despite its themes of love and forgiveness, the Bible is not always a feel-good book. Parts of it are quite confronting and shocking. There is a lot of violence, war, death and tough justice. You may be challenged in your words, thoughts and actions. You may read things that make you uncomfortable and may not quite fit in with your picture of God or what the Bible is all about. Some things seem unfair. Others you may have trouble understanding. Some of the great heroes of the Bible do terrible things and have pretty significant character flaws. Some of Jesus' teachings are difficult. The Bible pulls no punches. Make no mistake, the Bible is a serious book. It deals with serious stuff.

Third, Ben didn't really beat Pete in an arm wrestle.

*Then again, people have been reading biblical material for thousands of years without the benefit of this book, and Christendom seems to have got on well without us.

THANKS TO

Our Families

Thanks to Karen, Meredith, Rachael, Georgia and Matilda. Writing a book involves spending a lot of time away from your family and sitting in front of a computer screen. Thank you for your support and for maintaining interested expressions even when you were hearing the same bit read out for the tenth time.

Our Board of Advisors and Friends

Writing a book about the Bible is pretty daunting. On many occasions on the road between concept and finished product, we called upon a team of learned advisors and generous friends for feedback, comment, criticism, guidance, proofreading and advice. Thanks for giving us the thumbs up (or down) on our various ideas and chapters and for tolerating the occasional quirky and misguided thought with humour and grace. A lot of this book is thanks to you: Phil Andrew, Pat Antcliff, Ric Bollen, Peter Bolt, John Burns, Michael Frost, Steve Liggins, Simon McIntyre, Mick Martin, Julie Moser, Ken Moser, Phil Pringle, Bill Salier, Sue Salier, Mark Scott, Gavin Shume, Al Stewart, Andrew Tyndale and Graeme "Eagle Eye" Howells. None of them saw the final product before printing, so any heresies are ours.

Our Teachers

Over the past twenty years, we have both been privileged to learn from great teachers, preachers, leaders, lecturers and friends. These are Christian people who have taught us about the Bible at school, college, camp, beach mission, outreaches, concerts, Bible studies, church services, breakfasts, house parties and homes. To you, the multitude of nameless people, thanks for giving us a joy in the Bible, in Jesus and in the Christian life.*

Our Production Team

Thanks to our original production team in the form of Mamie Long and Anthony Wallace, and to John Dickson – author, evangelist, husband, dad and didgeridoo** player – for writing the foreword. (And thanks, John, for not writing this book!) Thanks to the team at Zondervan: to Stan Gundry for taking a chance on the new kids; to Katya Covrett for spotting us; to Brian Phipps and Lynn Wilson for helping us navigate the waters of mid-Atlantic style. And to Ron Huizinga and Tracey Walker for their work on the cover and the interior design.

*But this list does not include Ken, who shaved Pete's eyebrows once on a camp.
**An aboriginal musical instrument made of a hollowed log.

21

Part 1

THE GREAT JOURNEY

Try this quick quiz.

What Is It?

- It is a book, a best seller that most people on the planet have at one time read or at least casually glanced at.
- It has touched countless people with its insights and information.
- The English-language version is now distributed in over seventy countries.
- It opens doorways and tells us a lot about ourselves and our world.
- It is to be found in pretty well every library on the planet.
- It is available in thirty-seven foreign-language translations.
- Sales of this book are phenomenal, totalling somewhere up near the 100-million mark worldwide.

And the name of the book?

What was that you said? The Bible? Sorry, no. Wrong. Do not pass Go. Do not collect two hundred dollars.

It is actually *Guinness World Records*. Now, the *Guinness* is a good read and has some pretty impressive sales figures. And it also contains life-changing information, like the fact that in 1998 some guy blasted a strand of spaghetti nineteen centimetres* from one nostril. On every measurable scale, however, *Guinness* is chicken feed when compared to the world's *best*-selling book, which is, as you already know . . . wait for it . . . trumpet fanfare, please! *(bup-dudda-bup, bup-bup-bup-baaaa)* . . . **the Bible.**

It has been translated into over 2,200 languages and dialects. As a point of comparison, the works of William Shakespeare have been translated into only 50 languages. Bible Societies are currently working in over 200 countries producing translations in almost 500 new languages. They distribute over 500 million Bibles and Bible portions annually.

In the past twenty years, over 100 million copies of the Good News Bible have been printed. In China alone, almost 2.5 million Bibles are distributed each year. Despite its "thees" and "thous" from the seventeenth century, 13 million copies of the King James Bible are sold every year – to say nothing of

*About seven and a half inches, for those of you not used to metric measures.

the umpteen other versions that are walking out of bookshops around the globe every second of every day.

In the past two centuries, an estimated 5 billion (yes folks, not thousand, not even million, but *billion,* with a B* – that's 5 with nine 0s after it) Bibles have been printed. Wouldn't you just love to be the publisher who signed up the contract for that print run!

These figures are pretty staggering. In fact, they are so big it almost defies comprehension. So think of it like this: for about the past two hundred years, a Bible has been sold every few seconds of every minute of every hour of every day. At the same sales rate, the *Guinness World Records* would have sold out after only a few years.

If you were to stack these Bibles one on top of each other, you would have a tower 78,000 kilometres** tall. It would take the space shuttle travelling at full tilt over two hours to get to the top of the tower, and if the tower ever fell over, it would knock the earth out of orbit and start another ice age.

Or think of it like this: if you were to lay all these Bibles end to end in a single line, they would ... well, let's just say they would go lots and lots of times around the world and then make a three-lane bible-paved expressway up Mount Everest just because it was there. But the awesomeness of the Bible goes beyond simple sales figures. It is an awesome book that has had a critical impact on the shape of our world. For almost two thousand years, billions of people have been influenced by it, whether indirectly as the basis of law and morality in their country or directly as their personal guidebook to life, both physical and spiritual.

Half the people you know were probably named after someone in the Bible – like Matthew, Mark, Luke, John, Paul, ~~Ringo~~ ... Dan, Sarah, Eve, Adam, Mary, Jesus (if you live in South America), Rachel, Liz, Becky, Debbie, Mike, Zac, Joe, Josh, and on top of that, who doesn't know at least one Maher-Shalal-Hash-Baz.

- No other book even comes close to it.
- No other book is held in such high regard.
- No other book has been smuggled in so many car boots across dangerous borders.
- No other book has appeared so often in the top drawer of hotel bedside tables.
- No other book has been so widely studied (except maybe *Pride and Prejudice*).
- No other book has caused so much debate and controversy.
- No other book has been "sworn" over so much in courtrooms.
- No other book is so misunderstood by people who've never read it.
- No other book has had so many people living their life by it.
- No other book has had so many people who died for it.

> The Bible is an awesome book that has had a critical impact on the shape of our world.

Which leaves us with only one question: Why? Why is the Bible so popular, so translated, so widely read and so massively published? Because the pages make good cigarette paper? Don't think so. Because of the illustrations? No, because everyone knows Phantom comics have the best illustrations.

It is because the Bible tells us about God. If you were to put the Bible into a nutshell (you'd need a really big magnifying glass to read it), if you were to mortar and pestle it down into a single definition, it would be this:

The Bible shows us how to be in relationship with God.

Which is the biggest and most exciting topic of all time. But more of that in the chapters to come.

The Bible shows us how to be in relationship with God.

We, Ben and Pete, are both the proud owners of crusty old Bibles with pages falling out and the covers hanging on desperately. We got them when we were about sixteen, so we're a little attached to them in a nostalgic way.* Both Bibles are covered in grainy black leather and have three words printed on the cover: *The Holy Bible.*

> *Especially Pete. Given his age, his Bible is much older!   —Ben

Names often have meanings. *Ben*, for example, means "son of right hand", and *Peter* means "rock". But what do the words *The Holy Bible* mean? Before we even open the book, let's look at these three words.

The

Webster's Dictionary says that the definite article *the* is "used as a function word to indicate that a following noun or noun equivalent is a unique or a particular member of its class".

You may well say, *so what?*

One thing we can get out of this is that like *the* King, Elvis Presley, there is only one. Elvis was not *a* king. He was *the* King. The Bible is *the* Bible as opposed to *a* Bible. Sure, there are different language translations, but they're still *the* Bible. You can't go into a bookshop and say, "Hey, have you got that Bible in stock, the one where Jesus doesn't die but goes on to be a successful sailor with his own Mediterranean ferry company? No? Um . . . what about the one where Noah discovers crop circles in Mesopotamia?" There aren't lots of Bibles. There is only *the* Bible.

Holy

If something is *holy*, it is special to God. It is considered to be sacred and set apart for a special task. It belongs to God and is of great spiritual worth.** The Bible is not just any old book. It is a *special* book from God. Its writings are considered significant, sacred and important.

The Bible gives us insight into who we are, why we're here, what our purpose is and what the future is all about. It is a book of real truth that can change your life like no other. You won't find *that* in a lifestyle magazine.

**This does not explain, however, why Robin always used to say "Holy Smoke!" whenever Batman was handcuffed to a bomb with a sizzling fuse.

Bible

Some people think that the word *Bible* is some sort of special mysterious name. Not so. The word *Bible* comes from the Latin translation of the Greek word *biblia,* which simply means "books". The singular *biblos* ("book") was the name given to the outer coat of a papyrus reed, which was used in Egypt as writing material. By the second century AD, Christians were using this word to describe their special writings. It's the same word root that gives us *bibliography* (which is a list of books) and *bibliophile* (who is a lover of books). *Biblos*, however, does not give us the word *bib*, which is an item of protective clothing for toddlers at mealtimes and has nothing to do with God or books or anything like that.

In contemporary usage, a "bible" is a book that has authority, one that you can't do without. People refer to the Jimi Hendrix riff book as "the guitar player's bible" or the guidebook to the Appalachian Trail as "the camper's bible". Some books even put the word *bible* in their title to make them sound important, like *The Consumer's Bible: A Guide to Nontoxic Household Products* or *The Survival Bible: Surviving a Nuclear Winter*, but let's face it, these are just silly bibles.

So there you have it. The Holy Bible is ***God's one and only special book.***

Wow! And we haven't even got past the cover yet – and that, of course, is where all the good stuff lies.

> The Bible is God's one and only special book.

Okay, we're past the front cover and into the table of contents. Two things are immediately apparent:

- The Bible is broken up into two main sections, the Old Testament and the New Testament.
- The Bible is made up of sixty-six individual pieces of writing (called "books"), some of which have foreign-sounding and mysterious titles.

Before we go any further, let's look at these two features.

The Two Sections: The Old Testament and the New Testament

Granted, "The Old Testament" and "The New Testament" are not wildly creative titles. A modern publishing company would probably call the two parts of the Bible something more exciting, like "War and Peace: The History of Israel" and "Baby Born in Shed Saves World". But at least you get the idea that the Bible is in two bits – an older bit and a newer bit.

The words *old* and *new* are pretty straightforward: *old* meaning "having existed for a long time" or "from long ago", and *new* meaning "of recent origin".*

The word *testament* is a translation of an ancient Greek word that referred to a body of writing written by a person or a group of people who witnessed something important. Hence, the word *testify*.

Another way of referring to the Old and New Testaments is "the old covenant" and "the new covenant". The word *covenant* simply means "agreement", or if you want to be really colloquial, "deal".

> *Hence, we might refer to Pete as an old man and Ben as a new man.
> – Ben
>
> Or alternatively, Pete as mature and Ben as immature.   – Pete

The Old Testament

The Old Testament is made up of the thirty-nine older books of the Bible that testify to and record the events before Jesus was born in what we refer to as BC times (before Christ). It describes the "old deal" that God had with the people of earth in the early days of human history.

The Old Testament begins with the origin of the world and the creation of the human race but quickly focuses on God's dealings with one particular family who would over time become the nation of Israel. To save the human race, God makes a covenant, or deal, with the people of Israel and continues to renew this deal through a number of key leaders, such as Moses. The essence of God's old deal was that he would be their God and would bless them and give them a place to live. In return, they were to honour him and be an example to the rest of the world so that all people would come to know and worship God. God gave the Israelites rules (or commandments) to live by and regulations relating to good living and worship.

The Old Testament then pretty well follows the history and religious life of ancient Israel, covering a fifteen-hundred-year period, from about 1900 BC to 400 BC. During these fifteen hundred years, the Israelites have their good and bad moments as they endeavour to keep God's commandments and honour his deal. But eventually they come unstuck and fail to honour their side of the deal with God in numerous ways. In complete contrast, God remains faithful to the Israelites and honours each of his promises.

The latter part of the Old Testament tells of the adventures of a number of God's messengers, or prophets, who went around telling people to stop ignoring God and get back with the plan.

The New Testament

The New Testament is made up of twenty-seven books that testify to and record the events of Jesus' life and ministry and the spread of the Christian faith in the first century of what we refer to as AD times (from Latin *Anno Domini*, meaning "in the year of the Lord"). It describes the "new deal" that began when Jesus arrived on the scene.

This deal wasn't reserved for a particular family or nation but was, and continues to be, for the whole world. The new deal (as described in the New Testament) meant that the old deal (as described in the Old Testament) was over and a whole new set of circumstances had begun. The main thing to know here is that because of Jesus' life, death and resurrection, anyone could be "mates with God", not by keeping a set of commandments and rules, but by honouring Jesus as Lord and Saviour. This was a big deal! The New Testament narrates the start of this new deal with four books (called Gospels), which tell of the birth, life, teachings, miracles and death of Jesus. The Gospels also tell of how Jesus came back to life after he was executed. This is referred to as the *resurrection*.

Jesus lived and travelled in the same place that we read about in the Old Testament, and his travels were confined to an area about 190 kilometres long and 65 kilometres wide.*

The latter and larger part of the New Testament is made up mostly of letters of correspondence between an important Christian leader named Paul and the new Christian churches. In these letters, we learn a lot about life in the

The main thing to know here is that because of Jesus' life, death and resurrection, anyone could be "mates with God".

*About 120 miles by 40 miles.

first century and what it means to be a follower of Jesus Christ, or if you like, a "Christian". The letters discuss things like faith, persecution, encouragement, unity, wrong teachings, Jesus and holy living, to name a few.

As the followers of Jesus spread out into the world, so too does the focus of the New Testament. Paul travelled all over the Mediterranean region, to places familiar to us today, such as Syria, Turkey, Greece, Italy, as well as the islands of Crete, Cyprus and Sicily.

Deuteronomy, Zephaniah, Titus, Etc. . . . What the . . . ?

The Bible, although it is published as a single volume and sits on your book-shelf like any other book, is in fact more like an anthology.* It is a collection of sixty-six pieces of writing of various sizes, each of which is called a "book". But you may find yourself scratching your head at the strange and unusual titles of the sixty-six books. They're not called Book 1, Book 2, Book 3, Book 55, Book 66 or anything simple like that. Instead, they have enigmatic and unfamiliar titles, like Haggai, Job, 3 John, Revelation and Leviticus.

What is a *Haggai*?** Why are there three *Johns*? What do they all mean?

We are quite familiar with the use of titles for modern books, songs and films – *Titanic, Star Wars, Great Expectations, Bohemian Rhapsody, Harry Potter, Terminator, Waltzing Matilda, The Lord of the Rings, Mary Poppins, Yesterday*. Titles give us a frame of reference for a work and maybe tell us what it is about. The titles of Bible books are just the same.

Some of the titles are based on the book's *content.* So for example, the book of Exodus tells of the Israelites' exodus (departure) from slavery in Egypt, the book of Esther tells of a queen who helped save the Israelites in a time of trouble, the book of Acts tells of the acts (deeds, or perhaps even adventures) of some of Jesus' friends as they spread the word about Jesus, the book of Lamentations is a collection of poetic laments (expressions of grief) over the destruction of the city of Jerusalem in 586 BC.

Some of the books take their titles from their *author.* So, for example, the book of Daniel was written by Daniel, the book of Matthew was written by Matthew, the second book of Peter (2 Peter) was the second letter written by Peter, the book of Jude was written . . . you've got the point by now. Some of the authors have Hebrew names that are unfamiliar to us in the twenty-first century, like Habakkuk, Zephaniah, Malachi and Nahum. Not exactly the name of the bloke who lives next door, but people's names all the same.

Some of the books get their titles from the *people who received the piece of writing* in the first place. So, for example, the book of Romans is a letter from Paul to the church in Rome, the book of 2 Corinthians is Paul's second letter to the church in Corinth, the book of Titus is one of Paul's letters to his mate and coworker – no guesses here; that's right – Titus!

* However, The Holy Anthology doesn't quite have the same ring to it.
** No, it's not a Scottish dish of offal.

You will also notice that some of the books have a number in their title, like 1 Chronicles and 2 Chronicles, or 1 Peter and 2 Peter. Sometimes this means that they are separate documents. So for example, 1 Timothy and 2 Timothy are two letters from Paul written on different occasions to his friend Timothy.

Sometimes, however, the number designation in the title is for a more practical reason. 1 and 2 Samuel, for example, was originally one book. It was split into two by the translators of the **Septuagint,*** probably because it was too big to fit onto one scroll. This is much in the same way that in big cities, the telephone directory is split into two (A – K and L – Z) because otherwise no one would be able to lift it.

We go into the various books of the Bible in detail in part 2 of this book. But right now, let's answer the question, ***Who wrote the Bible?***

Chapter 4

AUTHOR, AUTHOR!

Who wrote the Bible?

There are lots of misconceptions about who wrote the Bible. Some people think that God gave the Bible to Moses on stone tablets, accompanied by copious amounts of smoke, fire, clouds and singing of choirs, just like in the movies. But God didn't give the Bible to Moses.

Some people think that Jesus wrote the Bible, or at the very least, dictated it to his followers as he travelled around the Mediterranean countryside wearing a white bathrobe while eating locusts and pomegranates. No. Some people think that the Bible was written by a roomful of boring old monks sitting around in a monastery. But while the monks made copies of the Bible (no photocopiers in those days, folks!), they weren't the original authors. Others believe it was written by one of the great characters from the Bible itself, like Adam, Noah, or Serug, father of Nahor. It wasn't.

Cynics may even suggest that the Bible was written by a conspiratorial group of thirteenth-century church leaders to oppress the masses, spoil everybody's fun and make up a whole lot of rules just for the heck of it, thereby propagating middle-class values and maintaining social control. Wrong again. So who wrote the Bible?

The fact is that no one person wrote the Bible. Nor, for that matter, was it written in a single lifetime. When we wrote the book you are holding, we had an idea, then we sat down at our computers for a few months until it was all done. The Bible was *not* written like this. The sixty-six books that make up the Bible were written by a multitude of authors, spanning a period from about fourteen hundred years before Christ to about sixty years after his death. You will recall from the last chapter that these books are grouped into two sections. The thirty-nine books in the Old Testament were written between 1400 BC and 400 BC, while the twenty-seven books in the New Testament were written over the sixty-year period after Jesus' death.

Because the Old Testament was written so long ago, there's some uncertainty about who penned some of the books. Moses is thought to have written five of them, and King David wrote many of the Psalms. A whole bunch of guys, like Isaiah, Jeremiah and Hosea, among others, are responsible for some of the latter parts of the Old Testament.

> The sixty-six books that make up the Bible were written by a multitude of authors, spanning a period from about fourteen hundred years before Christ to about sixty years after his death.

In the New Testament, a tax collector named Matthew, a scribe named Mark, a doctor named Luke* and a Mediterranean fisherman by the name of John wrote the famous four gospels. Luke also went on to write a sequel to his gospel – the book of Acts – which describes what happened to Jesus' friends in the years after his death.

A Roman citizen and Jew named Paul, who experienced a dramatic conversion to Christianity, wrote many of the New Testament books. Other books were penned by Peter and John (two of Jesus' mates) and Jesus' brothers, James and Jude.** Most of the writers led incredible and often inspiring lives, in periods of history that we can barely imagine. And sadly, many of them suffered terrible deaths because of their determination to spread the word about Jesus.

The writers of these sixty-six books were participants in the most extensive, successful and long-term writing project in history! Yet not one of them wrote their various pieces with the intention that they would eventually be published in a best-selling anthology called *The Holy Bible*. They were not commissioned by a publisher to write a piece "for an epic publication spanning the centuries that'll absolutely be a best seller"!

They were writing to specific people in specific historical settings about specific situations. Yet at the same time, their words speak to all people throughout the ages. While some of the writers knew their words would reach many people, not one of them had even the faintest whiff of a notion that a few thousand years from then, people all over the world would be poring over their words in the biggest-selling book of all time.

> The biblical writers wrote to specific people in specific historical settings about specific situations. Yet at the same time, their words speak to all people throughout the ages.

While some writers recorded biblical events as histories to be read by a vast range of people, many had no idea that their writings would actually be published at all. In fact, publishing as we know it didn't even exist back then! Most of the biblical writings are historical narratives. Some are collections of poetry, songs and wise sayings. Some are letters – much like you might write a letter to a friend or send a group email today.

The books were brought together many years later and put into the whole that we now know as *The Holy Bible*, much in the same way as a *History of Rock* compilation CD box set is made up of a range of songs from different bands over many years.

So, to summarize: the Bible is a collection of different "books" written at different times by different authors from different places in different styles and in different languages and with different audiences and different purposes. But (yes, there's always a "but") the Bible has a unique characteristic. Here it is on the next line, in colour, so you can't miss it:

There is a unity to the Bible.

To get back to our earlier example, the *History of Rock* CD box set is composed of a selection of random songs that in no way relate to each other. Other songs could replace them, and it wouldn't really make any difference (except for classics like "Stairway to Heaven" and "Bohemian Rhapsody").

The books of the Bible, however, make up a continuous, meaningful and unified whole. Although at times they are not chronologically arranged, they do fit together, each chipping in to narrate one giant story that threads its way from cover to cover. They are related to each other, give meaning to each other and even refer to each other.

Think of it like a jigsaw puzzle, where every piece fits in with another piece. Each piece has its own picture or design on it, but its full value only becomes apparent when it joins with the others to make a bigger picture. Each part is crucial to the overall picture, and when you put all the pieces into place, you get a picture of the central and most significant person of the Bible, Jesus. Or think of it as an epic history, in which different authors have each contributed their part to the overall narrative. Or think of it as a soup, with a variety of different vegetables and meats which together . . . um . . . okay, you've got the point.

Combined into what we know as the Bible, these writings reveal things about God that we otherwise wouldn't know and give a sweeping and magnificent account of God's dealings with the world and his people, from creation, through the growth and development, trials and tribulations of the nation of Israel, to the life of Christ and the start of the Christian church.

If we are going to have a chapter like this on the authors of the Bible, then there's one really important thing – perhaps the *most* important thing – left to cover. You see, the authors of the Bible had a secret coauthor guiding them and working with them.

This coauthor inspired the various authors and yet allowed them to write in their own styles, with their own literary idiosyncrasies (their emotions, language, backgrounds, writing styles, sense of humour) coming through.

The coauthor and writing partner was none other than God. For this reason, the Bible is referred to as the "inspired Word of God". As such, it has authority. This idea comes through in the Bible itself. For example, Paul wrote in a letter to Timothy, "All Scripture is God-breathed and is useful for teaching, rebuking, correcting and training in righteousness, so that all God's people may be thoroughly equipped for every good work" (2 Timothy 3:16–17). On another occasion, Peter wrote in a letter that "above all, you must understand that no prophecy of Scripture came about by the prophet's own interpretation of things. For prophecy never had its origin in the human will, but prophets, though human, spoke from God as they were carried along by the Holy Spirit" (2 Peter 1:20–21).

What does this mean in real terms? It means that the writers of the Bible didn't just make it all up off the top of their heads. God was inspiring them

> The books of the Bible make up a continuous, meaningful and unified whole. They are related to each other, give meaning to each other and even refer to each other.

The Bible was written by both man and God. It is inspired. It has authority. It is human. It is divine.

to write, and through this, God was able to reveal himself, his will and his purposes.

On the other hand, it doesn't mean that God took over the writers' bodies like in some B-grade sci-fi movie. The authors didn't suddenly go stiff, with their eyes rolling back in their heads and their jaws hanging slackly, while their pens mysteriously raced around the page, leaving behind secret messages from God, and when they woke up the next morning with a completed manuscript in their own handwriting thought, "Hey, how'd that get there?" No. Not like that at all. What it means is that the Bible was written by both man and God. It is inspired. It has authority. It is human. It is divine. Which makes it the most unique book on the planet.

Chapter 5

IT'S ALL GREEK TO ME

In what languages was the Bible originally written?

A lot of movies have been made about the Bible and biblical characters. There are the standard movies about Jesus that get wheeled out on TV every Christmas and Easter. And there are the classic epics with tantalising titles like *Samson and Delilah, The Ten Commandments, The Robe, Ben Hur, The Greatest Story Ever Told* and all 174 minutes of the uncreatively named *The Bible*. In these movies, tanned American actors with square jaws and steely blue eyes play the good biblical characters. And the bad biblical characters are played by British Shakespearean actors with pronounced accents and pointy beards, saying dramatic things like, "Take him away, Darius!"

When you see American actor John Wayne as a Roman centurion muttering the line, "Truly this man was the Son of God", it's easy to develop a subconscious belief that people living in the times of the Bible spoke English and that Jesus spoke English, as did the disciples and the Romans and all the big-league heavies of the Old Testament, like Moses, Daniel, David, Abraham, Noah, Adam and Eve and, yep, even God. You don't realise how silly this idea is, until you see a Bible movie in *another* language.

One night Pete was watching late-night television, and he stumbled onto an old French film about Jesus. At one point, Jesus saw his friends approaching on a dusty street and said to them, "Bonjour, ca va?" Pete sat bolt upright at the absurdity of this. *Jesus speaking French! How ridiculous! Jesus didn't speak French, for goodness sake!* But in reality, this is no more ridiculous than assuming that Jesus spoke modern English.

When Jesus walked out in the street and chatted with friends and preached sermons, he spoke the local language – Aramaic. If you went to see Mel Gibson's popular film *The Passion of the Christ*, you would have heard this language in use. Fortunately, the movie had English subtitles.

The Old Testament was written almost entirely in a language known as biblical Hebrew. The easiest way to hear what **biblical Hebrew** sounds like is to rent a *Star Trek* DVD and listen to the Klingons when they speak. Hebrew was considered a sacred and special language, but by the time of Jesus, it had become something of a lost and antiquated language to the average person in

> It's easy to develop a subconscious belief that people living in the times of the Bible spoke English.

For example, when Jesus read the Old Testament (as he did in Luke 4:16–20), he most likely would have been reading in Hebrew, and the words he read would have looked like this:

בראשית ברא אלהים את השמים ואת האר

– Genesis 1:1 in Hebrew

But while Jesus read in Hebrew, most of the local Aramaic speakers would not have had that language background.**

Four hundred years passed in the gap between the Old Testament and the New Testament. And in that time, something happened that would significantly change the spoken and written languages of the region.

About three hundred years before Jesus was born, a Greek leader, Philip II of Macedonia, gave command of his army to his son, Alexander the Great. (When he was given command of the army, he hadn't actually become "Great" yet. Back then, he was still known to his friends as "Alexander the Mediocre".) You may already be familiar with Alexander if you saw Oliver Stone's controversial 150-million-dollar epic, appropriately titled, *Alexander*.

Alexander led an aggressive military campaign, which achieved the spread of Greek rule until the Greek Empire was the biggest the world had ever seen. From all over the Greek-speaking world, soldiers brought their own regional Greek dialects to the melting pot of Alexander's army, with the Athenian dialect being particularly influential. A new blend of Greek began to emerge. This in turn was adopted and adapted by local populations until this dynamic new variety of Greek became the standard language of commerce, diplomacy and administration throughout the conquered regions. This new form of **Greek, called *Koine*,***** became the dominant dialect after the fourth century BC.

Because so many Jewish people no longer spoke Hebrew, Greek translations of the Old Testament writings began to appear. The Septuagint, meaning "seventy", so named because of the traditional belief that seventy scholars translated it from Hebrew into Koine Greek, was the most popular and authoritative of these. This work took place in the Egyptian city of Alexandria around 250 BC to 150 BC. A few hundred years later, Greek was still the dominant language, and as such, the New Testament writings were composed in Koine Greek.

GREEKWASORIGINALLYAVERYDIFFICULTLANGUAGETOREAD. Oh, sorry . . . we didn't suddenly break into Swedish. What we meant to say is Greek was originally a very difficult language to read. This is because, like our sentence above, it was originally written in capital letters, without punctuation or spaces. In addition, (of no great significance, but interesting if ever asked at a trivia night), Greek was originally written, like Hebrew, from right

*The synagogue was the Jewish name for the local centre for prayer, worship and study of the law, as well as a building used for local government and schooling. There was only one temple in Jerusalem, but each community had its own synagogue.
**A good analogy is audiences today watching opera in Italian. Just like most of us today would scratch our heads at an aria, the people in the synagogue in the time of Jesus would not have understood Hebrew.
***Pronounced COY-nay, which means "common" or "shared".

to left. Then for a period it was written in alternating directions: one line right to left, next line left to right, like ploughing a field.

THGIROTTFELMORFNETTIRWSAWKEERGCB005DNUORAMORF ... um, sorry ... let's try that again. From around 500 BC, Greek was written from left to right, probably as a matter of convenience to stop right-handed writers from smearing their work. When John was writing his account of Jesus' life in Koine Greek, this is what his words would have looked like:

ΟΥΤΩΣΓΑΡΗΓΑΠΗΣΕΝΟΘΕΟΣΤΟΝΚΟΣΜΟΝΩΣΤΕΤΟΝ
ΥΙΟΝΤΟΝΜΟΝΟΓΕΝΗΕΔΩΚΕΝΙΝΑΠΑΣΟΠΙΣΤΕΥΩΝΕΙΣ
ΑΥΤΟΝΜΗΑΠΟΛΗΤΑΙΑΛΛΕΧΗΖΩΗΝΑΙΩΝΙΟΝ

– John 3:16 in Greek

For most of us today, Hebrew and Greek look like ink-dipped mice have walked across a page. Thankfully, the Bible has since been translated into our everyday language so we can read and understand it. But how the Bible was, and is, translated is a big topic in itself, so we'll leave that for the next chapter.

Chapter 6

TO CRAUNCH A MARMOSET
How is the Bible translated into modern English?

When you read the Bible, you are not reading the original words, but a *translation* of those Hebrew and Greek words into your language. Translating from one language into another, however, is not always easy.

Take, for example, the case of José da Fonseca and Pedro Carolino who, according to Stephen Pile's *Book of Heroic Failures*, penned the definitive work in poor translation. Fonseca and Carolino's work, *English As She Is Spoke: The New Guide of the Conversation in Portuguese and English*, a phrase book for Portuguese holidaymakers, was published in 1855. Fonseca and Carolino were obviously determined men. They didn't let the insignificant fact that they spoke no English get in their way. Abundantly resourceful, they used a Portuguese-to-French dictionary and then a French-to-English dictionary to tailor their essential holidaymaker phrases.

Imagine the scene as Portuguese tourists descended on London, armed optimistically with phrases such as "This hat go well", "She make the prude", "For to wish the good morning", "Here is a horse who have bad looks", "That which feel one's snotly blow, blow one's nose" and "Do you cut the hairs?"

For the more intellectual traveller, the authors also provided some famous English proverbs and sayings, such as "The dog than bark not bite" and "The stone as roll not heap up not foam", as well as the gem "to craunch a marmoset" – which we don't even want to think about.

The challenge for any translator is to remain true to the original text and present it accurately, while at the same time making it accessible to the modern reader in contemporary language.

Even today, languages that are almost identical sometimes need translation. Pete found this out a couple of years ago when one of his "Australian" books was published in America. He had to rewrite it so it made sense to the American audience. Many words and ideas had to be "translated". Nappies became diapers. The family Tarago became the family minivan. Words like *colour* and *labour* were respelled as *color* and *labor*. References to Sydney Harbour, Australian ex-Prime Minister Paul Keating and the TV show *Sylvania Waters* had to be "Americanised". Even in this book you see occasional notes.

> The challenge for any translator is to remain true to the original text and present it accurately, while at the same time making it accessible to the modern reader in contemporary language.

The task for Bible translators is much more difficult, as they strive to build a bridge between cultures and languages that are thousands of years apart. On the one side: ancient languages in strange script that tell us about a couple of millennia worth of Jewish history in a corner of the Mediterranean basin in a time incredibly distant to us, a time before electricity, before industry, before Elvis and aerosol cheese, a time when the neatest technological innovation was a donkey pulling a cart. And on the other side of the bridge: the Internet-driven dial-a-pizza cable-TV-saturated disposable me-generation space age of the modern let's-do-lunch English-speaking hey-is-that-my-mobile-phone-or-yours? world. What a task!

It's hard enough explaining to a foreign tourist how to get to the nearest bus stop, let alone trying to translate several hundred pages of complex history, narrative, poetry and abstract concepts in a way that is meaningful to a modern reader.

So How Exactly Is the Bible Translated?

Translation fundamentally involves swapping a word (or cluster of words) from one language with a matching and equivalent word (or cluster of words) from another language. For example, *cheese* in English equals the French word *fromage*. *Yes* in Japanese is *hai*. *Blue* is *biru* in Indonesian. The German phrase *Ich liebe dich* can be translated word for word as "I love you".

One way of translating the Bible is to do it literally, where you pretty well translate **word for word** (with obvious adjustments made for grammar and punctuation, etc.). The King James Version, Revised Standard Version, American Standard Version, New Revised Standard Version, New King James Version and New American Bible are examples of Bibles that were translated word for word. This is fine for simple words and concepts. But it becomes more difficult when translating complex or abstract text. Let's look at a few of the issues involved in translation.

Finding an Equivalent Word

Sometimes a word that exists in one language may not have a simple match in another language. Bible translators have to work out how to deal with words or ideas that don't have easy partners in their own language. They have to present ideas and concepts in a way that makes sense to a modern reader, while remaining true to the original writer's meaning.

A good example comes from the first chapter of the book of Philippians (which was a letter written by Paul to his friends in the Roman colony of Philippi). In chapter 1, verse 27, Paul uses a word that was very important to the Philippians and to Roman culture in general. In his letter, Paul encourages his friends in Philippi literally to "citizenise themselves".

This is all well and good if you were a Philippian living two thousand years ago, when everyone was going around citizenising themselves left, right and centre and everyone knew what it meant. Roman citizenship was a very important part of the Philippians' sense of who they were, because of the great benefits of being associated with Rome. But this word means nothing in modern English and it has no counterpart in our cultural identity. So Bible translators have to convey its meaning using other words, in this case, "conduct yourselves in a manner worthy of the gospel of Christ" (Philippians 1:27 NIV).

Grammar

Consider this sentence: *Unique together languages words have all own called putting their into way sentences units of meaningful.*

Now let's rearrange that: *All languages have a unique way of putting their words together into meaningful units called sentences.* Sure, all the right words might be there, but if they're not arranged in the right sequence, they won't make sense. Translators have to consider this.

Look at this example based on the original Hebrew word order from the Old Testament.

> The heavens [are] recounting the honour of God, and the work of His hands the expanse [is] declaring.
> Day to day uttereth speech, and night to night sheweth knowledge. There is no speech, and there are no words. Their voice hath not been heard. Into all the earth hath their line gone forth, and to the end of the world their sayings.
> — *Psalm 19:1–4 YLT*

As you can see, Hebrew grammar does not always translate smoothly into English. Most Bible translators have to resequence the original languages into an English grammar pattern so that it makes sense, the result being:

> The heavens declare the glory of God; the skies proclaim the work of his hands. Day after day they pour forth speech; night after night they display knowledge. They have no speech, they use no words; no sound is heard from them. Yet their voice goes out into all the earth, their words to the ends of the world.
> — *Psalm 19:1–4*

Aaahhh! That's better!

Punctuation and Format

In modern English, we are very familiar with full stops, question marks, speech markings and other forms of punctuation. The structure of the original writings of the Bible, however, was quite different than that of modern English.

It seems the original writers had an aversion to full stops. For example:

> And Peter and John were going up at the same time to the temple, at the hour of the prayer, the ninth [hour], and a certain man, being lame from

the womb of his mother, was being carried, whom they were laying every day at the gate of the temple, called Beautiful, to ask a kindness from those entering into the temple, who, having seen Peter and John about to go into the temple, was begging to receive a kindness.

– Acts 3:1–3 YLT

This sentence is enormous and confusing. However, this is nothing compared to Ephesians 1:3–14, which originally was one sentence containing 202 words! Some English translations of this sentence contain more than 260 words!* So translators have to create sentence units that make sense to us.

In other parts of the Bible, some translators rework repetitive passages into a more modern format. In the book of Numbers, for example, Moses goes into great detail describing his census of the names of the tribes of Israel and who the leaders were and how many people were in each tribe and what they ate for dinner and anything else you can think of.

The fairly direct King James Version translates the passage as:

And on the east side toward the rising of the sun shall they of the standard of the camp of Judah pitch throughout their armies: and Nahshon the son of Amminadab shall be captain of the children of Judah. And his host and those that were numbered of them, were three score and fourteen thousand and six hundred. And those that do pitch next unto him shall be the tribe of Issachar: and Nethaneel the son of Zuar shall be captain of the children of Issachar. And his host, and those that were numbered thereof, were fifty and four thousand and four hundred. Then the tribe of Zebulun: and Eliab the son of Helon shall be captain of the children of Zebulun. And his host, and those that were numbered thereof, were fifty and seven thousand and four hundred. All that were numbered in the camp of Judah were an hundred thousand and fourscore thousand and six thousand and four hundred, throughout their armies. These shall first set forth.

– Numbers 2:3–9 KJV

This is all well and good, but it's long and cumbersome and repetitive.

The Good News Bible formats the same passage in a way that is much more familiar to the modern eye:

On the east side, those under the banner of the division of Judah shall camp in their groups, under their leaders, as follows:

Tribe	Leader	Number
Judah	Nahshon, son of Amminadab	74,600
Issachar	Nethanel, son of Zuar	54,400
Zebulun	Eliab, son of Helon	57,400
		Total: 186,400

The division of Judah shall march first.

— Numbers 2:3–9 GNT

Note that the information is the same, but it is laid out in a format that is short, clear and more accessible.

Idiom

Idiom is a fancy word referring to the unique sayings and the way things are expressed in a particular language. Some words and phrases have multiple meanings, subtleties and uses that are totally unfamiliar to a foreign speaker.

Pete (the coauthor of this book, not the guy in the Bible) found this out a few years ago when he was travelling in Japan. He was with some French tourists on a headland and was looking out to sea at the choppy swell. Pete said to one bloke, "Look at those white horses", referring of course to the foamy wave crests on the ocean. This bloke was dumbfounded and immediately began scanning the local scenery for a herd of escaped albino equines.

"'Orses?" he said. "I zee no 'orses! Where are zees white 'orses, you zay?"

"No, not real horses," Pete said, pointing dramatically. "The white wave tops out there."

"Ah," he said, "you mean des moutons de mer?"

"Huh?" Pete said.

"Des moutons de mer!" he said. "Ze sheep of ze sea!"

"Sheep?" Pete said. "I don't see any sheep . . ."

And on it went . . .

The task for Bible translators is to take particular ways of saying things in Greek or Hebrew and make them meaningful for a modern reader. Here's a simple example:

> For in very deed, as the LORD God of Israel liveth, which hath kept me back from hurting thee, except thou hadst hasted and come to meet me, surely there had not been left unto Nabal by the morning light any that pisseth against the wall.
>
> — 1 Samuel 25:34 KJV

Now, here is the crux of the matter. The word-for-word translation of this passage (above) is absolutely correct. It is true and accurate and an exact transfer of what the original text says. But does it make sense to you as a modern reader? Probably not. Aside from the awkward grammar, what is all this about urination? The reference to those who "pisseth against the wall" is an ancient colloquial way of saying "men" (as that is something men do standing up), and in this particular context, it refers to Nabal's men.

Sometimes translators of the Bible have to decode what to us are unusual expressions so that we can understand what is meant. Added to that, they have

> Sometimes translators of the Bible have to decode what to us are unusual expressions so that we can understand what is meant.

to translate issues of grammar and word choice and punctuation. Some Bibles, therefore, are not translated solely using a *word-for-word* technique, but rather a ***meaning-for-meaning*** technique. Some Bibles that transfer meaning for meaning are the Today's New International Version, the New International Version, the Good News Bible and the Contemporary English Version.

Today's New International Version, with its balance between word-for-word and meaning-for-meaning translation, translates the above passage as:

> Otherwise, as surely as the LORD, the God of Israel, lives, who has kept me from harming you, if you had not come quickly to meet me, not one male belonging to Nabal would have been left alive by daybreak.
>
> *– 1 Samuel 25:34*

There is one Bible but three different ways of translating the original text and its meaning.

This meaning-for-meaning translation attempts to be accurate to the original while modifying and upgrading words, grammar, punctuation and idiom to make the most sense to the modern reader.

So far we have mentioned the *word-for-word* method of translation and the *meaning-for-meaning* method. The third type of translation is the ***paraphrase.***

The Living Bible, New Testament in Modern English and The Message are all examples of paraphrased Bibles. The paraphrase is the loosest and most liberal translation of the Bible. It is a loose reworking of existing English translations, rather than a direct translation of the original words and languages.

The paraphrase is often very readable, but in making it so, liberties are taken and accuracy can be sacrificed. There is a lot more interpretation on the part of the author, who retells things in his or her own way, rather than closely following the original texts. As such, serious Bible readers generally use paraphrases only to add colour and texture to their understanding.

What we are left with, then, is one Bible but three different ways of translating the original text and its meaning. In the next chapter, we will have a more in-depth look at and comparison of the three different translation methods.

Chapter 7

NOT WRONG . . . JUST DIFFERENT
How do the three translation methods compare?

Think of the three translation methods as being on a sliding scale. At one end is the *word-for-word* method, which scores very high on textual accuracy but does not necessarily do so well when it comes to ease of reading and meaning. At the other end, we have the *paraphrase*, which gets maximum marks for readability, but often at the cost of original textual accuracy. And somewhere in the middle is the *meaning-for-meaning* method. None of these are arbitrarily better or more correct than the other; they are just different.

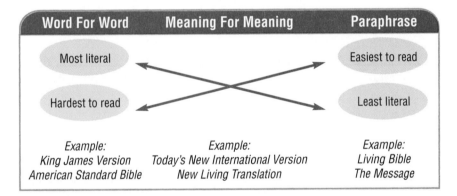

Word For Word   **Meaning For Meaning**   **Paraphrase**

Most literal   Easiest to read

Hardest to read   Least literal

Example:
King James Version
American Standard Bible

Example:
Today's New International Version
New Living Translation

Example:
Living Bible
The Message

A Final Word

The King James translation of the Bible came out in 1611. There are some Christians today who passionately believe that this word-for-word translation remains the ultimate English translation that cannot be surpassed. Books have been published on the subject. There are websites about the subject. There are surveillance satellites watching your house to see if you have any other Bibles besides the King James Version, and if you do, KJV commandos will raid your house and make you recite the book of Psalms in seventeenth-century verse. This obsession with a particular translation is arbitrary, to say the least.

The English language is constantly changing, and a few hundred years from now, the language we write and speak today will be as stiff and antiquated as the English language of Chaucer or Shakespeare is to us now.

> The English language is constantly changing, and a few hundred years from now, the language we write and speak today will be as stiff and antiquated as the English language of Chaucer or Shakespeare is to us now. There will never come a point when the "ultimate English translation" is written.

Here are some examples to compare the three translation methods.

Method	Word-for-Word	Meaning-for-Meaning	Paraphrase
Example	*King James Version*	*Today's New International Version*	*The Message*
Genesis 6:1	. . . men began to multiply	. . . human beings began to increase in number on the earth	. . . the human race began to increase
Exodus 25:23	. . . two cubits shall be the length thereof, and a cubit the breadth thereof, and a cubit and a half the height thereof.	. . . two cubits long, a cubit wide and a cubit and a half high.	. . . three feet long, one and one-half feet wide and two and one-quarter feet high.
1 Kings 2:3	And keep the charge of the LORD thy God, to walk in his ways, to keep his statutes, and his commandments, and his judgments, and his testimonies, as it is written in the law of Moses, that thou mayest prosper in all that thou doest, and whithersoever thou turnest thyself.	. . . and observe what the LORD your God requires: Walk in obedience to him, and keep his decrees and commands, his laws and regulations, as written in the Law of Moses. Do this so that you may prosper in all you do and wherever you go . . .	Do what GOD tells you. Walk in the paths he shows you: Follow the life-map absolutely, keep an eye out for the sign-posts, his course for life set out in the revelation to Moses; then you'll get on well in whatever you do and wherever you go.
Daniel 3:5	. . . that at what time ye hear the sound of the cornet, flute, harp, sackbut, psaltery, dulcimer, and all kinds of music, ye fall down and worship . . .	As soon as you hear the sound of the horn, flute, zither, lyre, harp, pipe and all kinds of music, you must fall down and worship . . .	When you hear the band strike up — all the trumpets and trombones, the tubas and baritones, the drums and cymbals — fall to your knees and worship . . .
Mark 6:31	Come ye yourselves apart into a desert place, and rest a while.	Come with me by yourselves to a quiet place and get some rest.	Come off by yourselves; let's take a break and get a little rest.
Luke 19:13	. . . delivered them ten pounds	. . . gave them ten minas	. . . gave them each a sum of money
John 11:39	Martha, the sister of him that was dead, saith unto him, Lord, by this time he stinketh: for he hath been dead four days.	"But, Lord," said Martha, the sister of the dead man, "by this time there is a bad odor, for he has been there four days."	The sister of the dead man, Martha, said, "Master, by this time there's a stench. He's been dead four days!"
Acts 3:1	Peter and John went up together into the temple, at the hour of prayer, being the ninth hour.	One day Peter and John were going up to the temple at the time of prayer — at three in the afternoon.	One day at three o'clock in the afternoon, Peter and John were on their way into the Temple for prayer meeting.
Romans 16:16	Salute one another with an holy kiss.	Greet one another with a holy kiss.	Holy embraces all around!

There will never come a point when the "ultimate English translation" is written that will be used for the rest of time. Bible translations will have to keep changing to reflect the common language and spoken tongue of the day.

When the King James Version came out in the 1600s, it was written in everyday language. But that language has now changed, and there are many words in it that are no longer used. The grammar has a quaint ring to it, and the words can seem awkward to us. (This is satirised in the cartoon *The Simpsons*. Whenever Homer goes to church, Reverend Lovejoy always reads some obscure long passage from the King James Version, and the congregation falls into a catatonic stupor!) Sure, from old hymns, you're probably familiar with words like *thee, thy, thou, art, ye, hallowed, believeth* and *verily*. But how many times a day do you use words like *almug, trow, chapt, habergeon, hosen, ligure, pate, ring-straked, trode, chode, wimples, ouches, tatches, brigandine, nard, purtenance, bruit, ambassage, cracknels, nusings, corban, charashim, gat, quarternion, wot, kab* and *sod* (and *pisseth*, for that matter!)? For this reason, many modern Bible readers tend to prefer more contemporary Bibles like Today's New International Version, the New International Version or the New Living Translation, which use words from our modern vocabulary.

The theory underlying the translation of biblical writings is complex, and we've just scratched the surface here. However, it's good to know some of the issues facing Bible translators. Language is an ever-changing entity, and the task of Bible translators is challenging and ongoing. Their main task is to present the Bible in a contemporary and meaningful way, weaving together words, grammar, idiom, layout and punctuation in a way that will make sense to readers in their own written language, while at all times maintaining the utmost accuracy and the integrity of the original text. Huge international teams – who are the best on the planet – do modern Bible translations, and it's reassuring to know that their methods are far superior to those utilised by José da Fonseca and Pedro Carolino!

So bruit your cracknels and let's chode into the next chapter, where we will purtenance the Bible's corban and discuss the writing materials of the Bible. This is totally amazing and habergeon and we hope the ambassage will bring you great wimples.

> The main task of Bible translators is to present the Bible in a contemporary and meaningful way that will make sense to readers in their own written language, while at all times maintaining the utmost accuracy and the integrity of the original text.

Let's try a little exercise.

In a few lines' time, you're going to read a word. It is the name of an object. When you read the word, close your eyes and picture that object on your mental screen.

Got it? Ready?

Okay, here it is. The word is *Bible*.

Hopefully, hours have not just passed and you haven't been sitting there with your eyes shut wondering what to do next. Perhaps we should have also instructed you to open your eyes after ten seconds and then keep reading. Anyway, what picture did you have in your head? Were you thinking of a shiny one-millimetre-thick silicon disk you can fit in one hand? Probably not. Yet that is exactly the Bible that we (as in Ben and Pete) sometimes use when finding verses.

If you're not up to speed yet, we're talking about the Bible on CD-ROM. You pop it into your computer and then access chapters and verses, do searches and a whole lot of other stuff.

Instead, you probably pictured a leather-bound book, perhaps with gold embossed letters (grandly stating *The Holy Bible*) on the front. The interesting thing is the Bible was not always a nice modern-looking book like that. When the biblical writings began their journey, books like those sitting on your bookshelf did not exist. In fact, paper as we know it didn't exist. Originally, the books of the Bible were written using a variety of different ancient materials.

The earliest writing material mentioned in the Bible is *stone*. Moses received the Ten Commandments on stone tablets (Exodus 24:12). Later on, in the book of Deuteronomy (27:1–8), instructions were given that stones were to be covered in lime or plaster, and then the words of the law were to be written on them. It is thought that the covering produced a surface that was easier to write on. It was common practice in the ancient world to set up stones inscribed with important messages.*

Another durable writing material common to the ancient world was *clay tablets.* These could be easily inscribed when wet and were virtually

> Originally, the books of the Bible were written using a variety of different ancient materials.

*Perhaps the most famous example is the Rosetta stone. Discovered by French soldiers in 1799, the Rosetta stone is a slab of black basalt inscribed in Egyptian and Greek in honour of the Egyptian pharaoh. It is thought to have been written by Egyptian priests in 196 BC and is now in the British Museum in London.

indestructible when dried or fired. Many thousands of clay tablets have been discovered throughout the Tigris-Euphrates River valley in the area that is now Iraq.

However, while stone and clay both were materials that would last a long time, they were not very user-friendly. They were bulky and heavy and not much use if you wanted to carry around a few Bible verses in your wallet. People must have got sick of taking a wheelbarrow full of Bible clay tablets with them every time they went to Bible study! In addition, there were potential dangers. For example, if you fell asleep while reading in bed, the tablet resting on your chest could fall forward and chip a tooth.

In Egypt, *papyrus* emerged as a popular and more user-friendly writing material. Papyrus, from which the word *paper* comes, is a reed plant that grows along the Nile River. The papyrus reed was cut into long strips and placed in alternating layers, vertically and horizontally. As the sheets dried, a natural sugar in the plant bonded the layers together, forming a rough, coarse ancestor of what we know as paper. It was easy to write on, was very light and could be joined together to create scrolls or pages. This early paper was fine in the Egyptian climate but was not well suited to much drier or wetter climates, where it rotted or disintegrated.

But wait, there's more! The skins of goats and sheep, in the form of tanned leather, were a pretty standard writing surface in the ancient world. But don't be thinking of leather like leather shoes or jackets. Animal skins, called *parchment,* were very fine. The skins were soaked in limewater, the hair was scraped off, and then the skins were dried and rubbed with chalk and pumice stone. The result was a fine, smooth writing surface. Extra-fine parchment was known as *vellum.* From about the second century BC, parchment and vellum seem to have taken over as the preferred writing material of choice.

All this talk of slabs of clay and sheets of parchment is fine when you are talking about a single "sheet" or short document. But what do you do when the document is lengthy? You can't just carry around a box of loose pages. They have to be put together in a meaningful way. Books as we know them weren't around when the Bible was being written. Instead, large documents were recorded in the form of a scroll.

A *scroll* was a continuous lengthy strip of animal skin rolled up onto two wooden rollers. Starting at the right hand side of the scroll (because Hebrew was written right to left), the reader would unwind the roller in their left hand and simultaneously roll it up with their right hand, while reading the page in the middle. (Much like town criers in period movies who read from scrolls, usually beginning with the words "Hear Ye! Hear Ye!")

There are over sixty references in the Bible to the use of scrolls. The first is when Moses is commanded to write on a scroll the account of his victory over the Amalekite army (Exodus 17:14). Jesus is described as reading from the

Books as we know them weren't around when the Bible was being written.

scroll of Isaiah (yep, the same as our Old Testament book of Isaiah) when he went to the synagogue (Luke 4:16–20).

Scrolls were records of very important information. They were treated with great care, often being sealed for protection, in much the same way that important books today might be put in a glass case in a library. They even had people whose special job it was to look after the scrolls in the synagogue. The scrolls of the ancient world were quite long. They could be almost a metre* wide. One of the Dead Sea Scrolls – the Temple Scroll – is partially damaged but had an original length of almost ten metres.** (We'll explain what the Dead Sea Scrolls are in the next chapter.)

But scrolls weren't very user-friendly. If you were at point A at the start of the scroll and you wanted to get to point B at the end of the scroll, you had to manually turn through the entire scroll in search of the relevant section. If you've ever fast-forwarded through a video looking for a specific scene, you know how time consuming and cumbersome this can be. Perhaps it was this difficulty that led people to seek an easier way of writing and reading long documents. Around the second century AD, a new type of formatting began to emerge. Enter . . . the *codex.* Sounds mysterious, doesn't it? In fact, it's something you're already familiar with. Look at the book you are holding in your hands. This is an example of the codex format; namely, a series of individual pages, stacked one on top of the other and bound on the left side. If you are at point A at the start of a book and you want to get to point B at the end of a book, you can get there immediately. Think of it like watching a DVD and being able to use the scene selection function to . . . well, you get the point.

For many hundreds of years, copies of the Bible were handwritten. In this age of PCs and word processors and photocopiers and voice-recognition software, it's hard for us to appreciate the enormity of this task. Each copy was meticulously reproduced and often elaborately decorated by professional scribes. It was time consuming and meticulous work. On top of that, if your copier ever died, you had to organise a funeral, not just tech support. The early 1400s, however, brought a revolution with the introduction of the first industry of mass production – book printing. Bibles could be produced quickly, and the Bible in its codex form exploded into the world. And that's the way it has been for hundreds of years until relatively recently with the arrival of the information revolution. Now you can get the Bible on CD or download it from the Internet.

Stone, clay, parchment, vellum, paper, digital code – the Bible has certainly been on a tremendous journey in terms of its medium of delivery. The important thing to note is that even though the *format* of the Bible has changed, and will continue to change, the *content* has not. It is as valid and relevant now as it has always been.

> Even though the *format* of the Bible has changed, and will continue to change, the *content* has not. It is as valid and relevant now as it has always been.

We can't begin to imagine what form the Bible will take five hundred years from now.

Ben has lots of Bibles, and one of them looks like a penknife. It's the same shape and size, and it has a pen-style clip for his pocket. This "Bible" is actually a ThumbDrive, in which Ben carries around all his electronic Bibles and Bible software. It plugs straight into his laptop via the USB port. That's pretty fancy today. We can't begin to imagine what form the Bible will take five hundred years from now, when all the trees are gone and there's no more paper or books and personal computers are as old-fashioned as telex machines. Who knows in what format people will be reading the Bible then? Perhaps it will be in three-dimensional holograms or light-fibre tubes or handheld crystal data projections or personal info-chip screens implanted under the skin of the forearm.

No matter how freaky that seems to us today, it is still reassuring to know that Bible readers in the future will know, as they have for the past two thousand years, that God loved the world so much, that he sent his son, Jesus, to die for us all (John 3:16).

Chapter 9

PUTTING THE PIECES TOGETHER
How was the official version of the Bible first put together?

By now, you might be asking some interesting questions. Maybe something like: "Okay, the Bible is a collection of sixty-six documents written over a fourteen-hundred-year period, right? (Right.) And it was written by God and a whole lot of human authors, right? (Right.) And nearly all of those authors had never even met many of the other authors, right? (Right.) And they had no idea that their writing would eventually be included in a single publication known as *The Holy Bible*, which would be the biggest-selling book of all time, right? (Right.) And Ben and Pete are experts in biblical history, geography, theology, archaeology and a whole range of other important 'ologies', right? (Well, no, not exactly. But let's not worry about that for the moment). Well then, hang on a sec . . . how did those writings come together to form the Bible? And is it true that a flea can jump 350 times its own body length? (How did that thought get in there?)"

To answer this question (the one about the Bible, not about the flea), let's go back in time. Back before the age of personal computers, mobile phones and TV dinners; before the days when Ben and Pete played in rock bands and had hideous haircuts;* back before the Model T Ford, the Wright brothers, Henry V, Marco Polo, Leonardo da Vinci; back before the telescope; back before the world was pizza-shaped; back to the age of Jurassic dinosaurs when T-Rex was king of the . . . Woah, too far. Come forward, forward. That's it . . . to the time when a bloke called Jesus-son-of-Joseph (a.k.a. Son of God) was growing up and learning his trade as a carpenter in a hot, arid country on the shore of the Mediterranean Sea, namely, somewhere around the time that we might think of as the year zero.

Back then, there wasn't a printed Bible as we know it. Not only would it be more than a thousand years before the printing press was invented, most of the events described in the New Testament hadn't happened yet.

Being a typical Jewish family, Jesus' parents – Joseph and Mary (known as Joe and Mazza to their friends) – would have taken him to the synagogue regularly. There they would worship, pray and listen to readings from the Jewish holy scriptures. These scriptures were a collection of writings, and each synagogue would have had its own meticulously handwritten copies.

> *Hey, I never had a hideous haircut! —Pete
>
> Oh yeah, when was the last time you looked at your wedding photo, Mullet Head? —Ben

When Jesus was a child, he would have sat in the synagogue and listened to selections of these writings being read out loud. Later, as an adult, he held the scrolls in his hands, read from them and taught in the synagogue.

Now, here's the interesting thing. That same collection of Jewish writings that Jesus read from in the synagogue is the same collection of Jewish writings that you have in the front part of your Bible, labelled the Old Testament. "Our" Old Testament already existed as a single entity over two thousand years ago.

There are three main ways we know this.

First, there are loads and loads and loads of instances in the New Testament when the writers quote the Old Testament. So they obviously knew it existed and were familiar with it. As we said, Jesus grew up with the Scriptures and quoted them frequently.

Second, the Old Testament was translated into Greek by a number of scholars in Egypt over two hundred years before Jesus was born.* Therefore, we know it existed as a single entity.

Third, two years after World War II finished, a shepherd was doing the whole goat-and-staff-thing when he stumbled across a cave near Qumran, an ancient settlement on the northwest shores of the Dead Sea. Inside the cave, he made the archaeological find of the century – a find worthy of the most action-packed Indiana Jones movie. Over the next nine years, scholars and archaeologists scoured the area and discovered hundreds of caves. Amazingly, eleven of them (five were natural and six were man-made) turned out to be filled with treasure. Not treasure like rubies and diamonds and padlocked chests overflowing with gold doubloons guarded by a feisty skeleton with an eye patch, but treasure all the same. The caves revealed a multitude of clay jars containing well-preserved scrolls of leather and papyrus, and even one made out of copper.

These Dead Sea Scrolls turned out to be a library; a complete collection of the Old Testament (except for the book of Esther), and dating shows that they were produced between 150 BC and AD 50. It is likely that the Jewish community at Qumran sealed and hid their precious writings in these caves to keep them safe from advancing Roman soldiers sometime around AD 70.

And there they sat for almost two thousand years.

"So what?" you may say. "What does this tell us?"

Well, it confirms that the Old Testament existed as a collection of writings at the time when Jesus was alive, over two thousand years ago. And on top of that, these sacred writings were part of everyday life and society.

Around AD 100, a group of rabbis (Jewish leaders) in Jamnia, Palestine, formally recognised the writings as the official version of the Hebrew Bible, which is what you know as the Old Testament. The term for the official version is the *canon.*

"So what about the New Testament?"

*See the next chapter for more details.

"Our" Old Testament already existed as a single entity over two thousand years ago.

After the Roman government executed Jesus, many accounts about his life and teachings were circulating. His followers spread out around the Mediterranean region, and gatherings of "Christians" continued to spring up everywhere in what were the earliest Christian churches.

The accounts of Jesus' life, teachings, death and resurrection – written by Matthew, Mark, Luke and John – were doing the rounds. So too were Paul's letters to various churches and friends, in which he addressed issues about Christian teaching and living. By the third century AD, these documents were widely circulated and used by Christian communities as writings of great significance. There were, of course, other writings around at the same time that were not held in such high regard. There were also other documents about Jesus' life, but they weren't considered to have the same authority.

By the second half of the fourth century AD, a collection of writings was recognized (or "canonized") by two official gatherings of Christian bishops at the impressive-sounding Council of Carthage and Council of Laodicea. Those writings are in your Bible. They make up the New Testament.

There you have it. After extensive periods of common usage, the various books of the Bible were officially sanctioned in AD 100 (Old Testament) and AD 363 (New Testament).

Even so, there are questions yet unanswered.

It would be over a thousand years before a German named Johann Gutenberg would sit up in bed one night and say, "Eureka! I've got an idea for a machine that will print books!"

So how did these early handwritten Hebrew and Greek copies survive the passage of time and make it onto your bookshelf in a mass-produced single volume almost two thousand years later?

Read on, MacDuff, and all will be revealed.

> After extensive periods of common usage, the various books of the Bible were officially sanctioned in AD 100 (Old Testament) and AD 363 (New Testament).

Chapter 10

JOURNEY THROUGH THE CENTURIES
How did the Bible cross the barriers of time and language?

In its life, the Bible has gone on an incredible journey.

Historically it has thrived for over twenty centuries while kingdoms and governments and armies and even entire nations have come and gone.

Geographically it has spread from humble beginnings in a few pockets on the shores of the Mediterranean Sea to every corner of the planet.

Linguistically it has multiplied from long-gone, ancient tongues into thousands of modern languages and dialects.

Tragically it has come to us at a great cost, with countless people dedicating their lives and suffering almost unimaginable persecution and death just so we could read the Bible in our own language.

The Bible has gone from handwritten parchment scrolls to being the most printed, widely read, biggest-selling book in history – and all this without the benefit of a public relations company, advertising campaign or mass media production team! But how did this all come about? How did the Bible make the journey into other languages?

The Early Centuries

In those early centuries after Jesus' death, the world encountered the biggest phenomenon it has ever seen – at least since that big comet landed in Manson, Iowa. Christianity moved outward from the Mediterranean region like an expanding ripple caused by . . . well, think of the effect of dropping a semi-trailer into a fish pond.

But the journey was not always smooth. The Christians – still a minority group – suffered the most terrible persecution and hostility for their beliefs. The Roman government did their level best to keep the whole Christian thing under wraps.

The psychopathic Emperor Nero and his regional governors were killing and torturing Christians as a matter of course during the first century. By AD 200, Emperor Severus prohibited the spread of Christianity, and some Christians were forced to participate in pagan religious ceremonies.

The deaths of Christians and church leaders continued, and by the start of the fourth century AD, Emperor Diocletian continued a massive reign of terror, enslaving Christians in work mines, executing and torturing them and throwing them in prison or the arena with nasty gladiators or even nastier wild animals. But despite the persecution, Christianity and the Bible continued to move out into the world.

Things improved greatly, though, when the Roman Emperor Constantine became a Christian in AD 312. The next year, together with Lucinius Augustus, he issued a law that allowed freedom of religion and returned stolen property to the Christians.

The Bible Goes Global

As you can imagine, after hundreds of years of repression, the "good news" of Christianity exploded out into the world, spreading like wildfire, from town to town, across borders and seas, down into Africa, over into the Middle East, north into the Russian states and northwest into Europe.

In the wake of this expansion, the followers of this new religion wanted access to its official documents and writings. Handwritten copies of parts of the Bible proliferated and were used for teaching and worship in the various Christian communities around the known world.

There are a lot of languages in the world, and it can be something of a struggle when dealing with a language that is not your own. Ben found this out the hard way a few years ago. Having just returned from a trip to China, he decided to try out some of his newfound linguistic skills at a Chinese restaurant. He greeted the waitress with a hearty *"Nihau!"* and instead of friendly Chinese banter by way of reply, was surprised to receive a sigh and a stony stare. A few awkward moments passed by. "Sir," said the waitress in a crystal clear English accent, "This is a *Korean* restaurant." Needless to say, Ben hasn't been back there since.*

People in those early Christian communities struggled with other languages too. Not all of them had conversational Hebrew, Aramaic and Greek under their linguistic belts.

And so the writings began their journey into other languages.

The Bible made headway south into Africa, starting with an Egyptian (called "Coptic") translation and eventually making it into Ethiopian and Nubian. Meanwhile, a Syriac translation got a foothold in the north and east, spreading up into the future southern Soviet states with translations into Georgian, Armenian and Old Slavonic.

Heading north and west into Europe, Latin was the common language of the Roman Empire, and so Latin translations began to appear. A scholar named Jerome consolidated the many emerging Latin translations into an official Latin translation (called the ***Vulgate,*** which means "common" Bible) in the

Despite the persecution, Christianity and the Bible continued to move out into the world.

*Thanks, Ben. Great story. A reminder: this is a book about the Bible. Your point is?
    – Pete

Stop being so impatient. You are very difficult to work with.   – Ben

Sorry. Nice segue.
    – Pete

late fourth century. He moved to Bethlehem to master the languages and then translated the whole Bible from Greek and then the Old Testament from Hebrew. His project took over twenty years. Soon the Christian church was strongly established, and Jerome's Latin Bible was used all over Europe. In fact, it would be the dominant Bible of Europe (including England) for over a thousand years. By AD 500, parts of the Bible had been translated into hundreds of languages and dialects. By the seventh century, the four gospels had made the difficult linguistic step into Chinese, closely followed by an Arabic translation. But there was still a long way to go.

New Translations Emerge

With the collapse of the Roman Empire in the fifth century, Latin ceased to be the all-encompassing and unifying language of Europe. And as it faded into oblivion, all the regional tribes and peoples of Europe re-established their own dialects and languages. And further translations of the Bible began to appear.

The Gospels appeared in early German (known as Frankish), while over in England, portions of the Psalms, the Ten Commandments, the Lord's Prayer and bits of the Gospels were emerging in Anglo-Saxon. One of the translators was the Benedictine monk, writer and scholar Bede (who also appeared as a character in an episode of the cult TV show *Dr. Who*). Another translator was King Alfred the Great, who, when he wasn't fighting off Danish invasions, had a passion for translating classical and historical literature.

As an interesting aside, it was around this time – at the start of the sixth century – that an Italian abbot by the name of Dionysius Exiguus began the system of dating time in relation to Christ's birth. Everything before Christ was counted backward and labelled "BC", meaning "before Christ", and everything afterward was labelled "AD", not meaning "after death" as some people believe, but rather the Latin *Anno Domini*, meaning "in the year of the Lord".

The real explosion in Bible translation, though, occurred in the second millennium, namely AD 1300 to AD 1600. The Bible was slowly emerging in a range of common European languages – early French (Provençal), Danish, Polish, Spanish, Italian, Serbian, Czech, even Icelandic.

But over in England, the church had totally failed to move with the times. Although Latin had long gone as the language of common use, the church clung to its Latin version of the Bible and used it exclusively. Church services, prayers and Bible readings were still conducted in Latin, which was fine for the few church leaders and highly educated scholars who could read and understand it. But for the ordinary people, this thing called *The Holy Bible* was read aloud in an ancient foreign language and, as such, was totally inaccessible. That is, until a Yorkshireman named John decided to translate it into English.

The real explosion in Bible translation occurred in the second millennium, namely AD 1300 to AD 1600.

An Early English Bible

In the late 1300s, John Wycliffe, a priest – and Oxford philosopher, lecturer, Doctor of Theology and inventor of bifocal glasses – decided that the Bible should be accessible to Mr and Mrs Average, not just Latin-speaking clergy. So in 1378, he and some of his Oxford Uni buddies (especially his friends John Purvey and Nicholas de Hereford) broke from tradition and began translating the Latin Bible into the ordinary English of the day. Four years later, they had finished their manuscript, and many hundreds of handwritten copies were made.

Here's an example of the first English version; Wycliffe's translation of the famous verse often waved about by people with bits of cardboard at major sporting events, John 3:16:

> Forsothe God so loued the world, that he gaf his oon bigetun sone, that ech man that bileueth in to him perische not, but haue euer lasting lyf.

Excuse me, did you say *English*? Well, yes, but the Middle English of the 1300s was different from the modern English we use in the 2000s. Back then, it was a hotchpotch of Anglo-Saxon, Latin and Norman, with a dollop of French, a splash of Greek, half a teaspoon of German and some Viking on the side, just for good luck.

Can you imagine what it must have been like, when after years of expectation and anticipation, the Bible finally came out in common English? Perhaps there would have been a lavish ceremony with the royal family and civic officials in attendance. Maybe a huge parade through London, with music and feasting and jugglers and performers on stilts and fireworks, and John Wycliffe knighted with much pomp and ceremony. Statues erected in his honour. Cities renamed after him. Public readings of God's Word in English. Imagine the celebration!

Sadly, it was not like this at all – quite the opposite. Rather than the English Bible being welcomed with open arms, it went down like a lead balloon. Amazingly, the fiercest opposition came from the church itself.

After centuries of having exclusive control over the Latin Bible, Wycliffe's English translation was a serious threat to the church's power. If the ordinary Joe in the street could read God's Word for himself, the church would lose its importance and its monopoly of the Bible. Its more shaky practices and teachings would be exposed as fraudulent. No longer would the church be able to justify unbiblical income gained by selling the forgiveness of sins or receiving donations to purchase souls out of a fictionalised purgatory. People would begin to challenge some of the church teachings about Mary and the pope. People would question the need for priests to forgive their sins and would challenge the elevation of church leaders to sainthood. People would realise that it was their faith, not their deeds or donations, that put them into a right relationship with God.

Rather than the English Bible being welcomed with open arms, it went down like a lead balloon.

Potentially, it was as disastrous as the proliferation of high-quality supermarket noodle kits has been to the Asian restaurant industry.

Consequently, in the early 1400s, some church leaders in Oxford banned Wycliffe's Bible. They considered it too dangerous for the uneducated masses to read the Bible. Many of the handwritten copies were burned, and punishments for owning a copy were severe. The strength of the church's dislike of this newfangled English Bible is evident in the fact that fifty years after Wycliffe died, the pope commanded that his grave be dug up and his bones crushed and dumped in the river!

So the English people still didn't have a Bible in their own language. But like a crack in a dam wall, Wycliffe had paved the way for other translators to follow.

The Mass Production Revolution

About fifty years after Wycliffe died, a little known German businessman, Johann Gutenberg, started toying with an idea. Within ten years, he had created the world's first industry of mass production: the printing press with movable type.

Gutenberg's wonderful new machine started a revolution that would change the shape of the world. Prior to that time, documents or books (including the Bible) had to be copied by hand, often with elaborate decorations on the pages. As you can imagine, this was a phenomenally time consuming, expensive, inefficient and laborious process. Because this process was so labour intensive, copies were expensive; a single copy cost the equivalent of six years of a labourer's wages. With Gutenberg's machine spitting out three hundred pages a day, what used to take a year could be done in a day. This paved the way for relatively quick and large-scale book production.

Gutenberg's first project was the Latin Bible, which took him six years to complete and was published in 1456. Over the next twenty years, printed Bibles would also come out in Italian, Dutch, Catalan (for Spain) and German. The invention of the printing press was a critical element in the Bible's journey to the masses. The only problem was there was *still* no readily available English version.

> The invention of the printing press was a critical element in the Bible's journey to the masses.

Chapter 11

AT LAST . . . AN ENGLISH BIBLE
How did God's Word break through to the English-speaking people?

A t the start of the 1500s, a priest, William Tyndale – also a Cambridge and Oxford scholar fluent in several languages – began a mission to give the ordinary people of England a Bible they could read. Like many scholars, he was increasingly dissatisfied with the Vulgate's monopoly on Bible readership. He said it was next to impossible for ordinary Christians to be strong in their faith "excepte the scripture were playnly layde before their eyes in their mother tongue".

The problem was the church still clung desperately to the Latin Bible, and the idea of a plain-English version evoked massive resistance. So in 1524, Tyndale left England and headed to Germany. There he met up with Martin Luther – theological mastermind and Doctor of Biblical Theology at the University of Wittenberg – who was busy working on his own German translation of the New Testament.

Using Jerome's Latin version, Luther's German and the original Greek, Tyndale translated the New Testament into English. Copies started arriving in England in 1526, smuggled across the English Channel like illegal contraband, in hay bales and sacks of corn and flour. Tyndale's Bibles were not popular with some church officials, who promptly burnt as many copies as they could get their hands on. The books were forbidden, and heavy punishments (a month in prison or even public execution) were imposed on people just for having one in their possession.

In 1535, while hiding out overseas and working on his translation of the Old Testament, Tyndale was arrested and held captive for a year and a half in a castle in Belgium. He was found guilty of heresy and was strangled and burnt to death in October 1536.

Another priest and Cambridge Uni graduate, Miles Coverdale, had also headed over to Germany in 1528. Using a lot of Tyndale's work, Coverdale published the first full English translation of the entire Bible, the *Coverdale Bible*, in Zurich in 1535.

Although men like Bede, Wycliffe and Tyndale weren't there to see it, their vision of a plain-English version of the Bible had at last come to reality.

> Although men like Bede, Wycliffe and Tyndale weren't there to see it, their vision of a plain-English version of the Bible had at last come to reality.

In Search of an Official Version

Aided by the printing press and a number of scholars dedicated to the task of bringing the Bible to the people, English translations began to pop up all over the place.

The *Thomas Matthew Bible* was the first English Bible to be printed in England, in 1537. This was published by one of Tyndale's colleagues, John Rogers, who used the pseudonym Thomas Matthew, perhaps to protect himself in the still unstable environment.

By 1540 the church decided that if you can't beat them, join them. The archbishop of Canterbury, Thomas Cranmer, commissioned Miles Coverdale to produce the first officially sanctioned English Bible. The *Great Bible,* so known because of its massive size, was placed in every church, chained to the lectern, and for a while, things looked promising.

The death of King Henry, however, heralded a new dark era for the English Bible. Queen Mary took the throne and promptly began executing hundreds of church reformers. In 1555, both John Rogers and Thomas Cranmer were burned at the stake. Many Bible scholars escaped across the Channel and took refuge in Europe. The Swiss city of Geneva became home for Miles Coverdale, who, together with other scholars, set to work on a new English translation. The *Geneva Bible* came out in 1560. It was the first Bible to have maps and tables and to insert verse references into the text. This was also the first Bible to use Roman script, much like what you are reading now.

The *Bishop's Bible* (named after the church bishops, who, still a bit miffed about the whole Bible translation thing, produced their own version) came out in 1568. They promptly ordered all churches to have a copy. The *Rheims New Testament* (1582) and *Douay Old Testament* (1610) followed, named after the towns in France in which they were printed. So by the start of the seventeenth century, there were quite a few English Bibles floating around, but no version was officially recognised.

Then, in February 1604, King James I of England declared it was time that the many English translations were superseded by a "modern" and official English Bible that would be acceptable to all of the Christian factions. He ordered "a translation be made of the whole Bible, as [close] as can be to the original Hebrew and Greek".

About fifty of the best scholars in the business promptly began the task, with two teams each working out of Oxford, Westminster and Cambridge. The result, published in 1611, was the *King James Version* – also called, for obvious reasons, the *Authorized Version.*

For the first time in history, one thousand six hundred years after Jesus was working through his carpentry apprenticeship, the English-speaking world

> By the start of the seventeenth century, there were quite a few English Bibles floating around, but no version was officially recognised.

had an official, reliable and readable Bible that was available to the ordinary folk in the street. The King James Version (KJV) would be the standard Bible of English speakers for hundreds of years. Even today, some Christians believe it is still the ultimate English Bible, far surpassing any more recent translations. You can still buy it in your local bookshop, and it still sells several million copies a year.

A Plethora of English Versions

For two hundred and fifty years, the King James Bible reigned supreme among English Bibles.*

Over the years, research into the original Bible manuscripts improved greatly. Scholars had a clearer understanding of the Hebrew and Greek, and archaeological discoveries had unearthed other original texts. In addition, the English language had changed, and many words in the KJV were no longer in common use.

So in 1870, the Bishop of Winchester proposed to a Church of England conference that a new revision of the Bible be made, incorporating advancements in language, scholarship and translation. Two teams of twenty-seven scholars were set up to revise and modify the KJV. Parallel teams were also set up in New York City to collaborate with the London teams and to comment upon suggestions and alterations.

In keeping with the theme of the editions of the Bible having blatantly obvious titles, this revised version was given the title – no prizes here, folks – the *Revised Version.* The New Testament was published in 1881, with the Old Testament following in 1885. Because of some linguistic differences, the Americans followed with the *American Standard Revised Version* in 1901.

The twentieth century, however, was when things really heated up for the Bible, with the production of more versions and formats than you can poke a stick at. Nowadays, there are red-letter Bibles, amplified Bibles, literal-translation Bibles, gender-accurate Bibles and paraphrased Bibles. There are Bibles with two versions in one and Bibles with all the verse references removed so they read like a normal book. There are Bibles on CD and audiotape, slim-line Bibles, braille Bibles, kids' Bibles and teenagers' Bibles. There are heaps of study Bibles that contain comments and notes and questions and essays to prompt discussion and research – there's a Leadership Bible, a Prophecy Bible, a Quest Study Bible and a Life Application Study Bible.

On the other hand, there are others that render the Bible as a story. Rob Lacey's *The Word on the Street* uses contemporary urban language – "just the way most people talk," Rob says – to communicate the story of the Bible to the modern reader. Or *The Story* – a condensed retelling of the stories, poems and teachings of the Bible using the text of *Today's New International Version* – which reads more like a novel than your typical religious text.

> Sixteen hundred years after Jesus' time, the English-speaking world had an official, reliable and readable Bible that was available to the ordinary folk in the street.

There's a dramatised Bible that sets out the entire Bible as a play (with a script and stage directions) and there are Bible paraphrases written out to appeal to specific subcultures, like Kel Richards' *The Aussie Bible*. And for people with really good eyesight, the Massachussets Institute of Technology produced a New Testament in microlithography on one sheet measuring just one-quarter of a centimetre* square. This, coincidentally, is also the Bible most likely to get lost!

Ultimately, these are all interesting ways of setting out the Bible that have various uses and appeals to specific audiences. But they all use only a small number of actual translations. Some of today's most popular English translations are: the *Revised Standard Version* (RSV, 1952), *JB Phillips New Testament* (Phillips, 1958), *New American Standard Bible* (NASB, 1963), *New English Bible* (NEB, 1970), *The Living Bible* (LB, also called The Book, 1970), *Good News Translation* (GNT, also called Good News Bible or Today's English Version, 1976), *New International Version* (NIV, 1978), *New King James Version* (NKJV, 1979), *New Revised Standard Version* (NRSV, 1990), *New Living Translation* (NLT, 1996), *Today's New International Version* (TNIV, 2005), as well as the large-print special Year 2000 edition of the Bible (the "Big Ultimate Millennium" version, whose acronym was BUM, which had its name changed for reasons unknown).

All of these are fair-dinkum** and real Bibles, and they all say the same thing. Each has its own style and wording, however, to suit the language of a particular audience.

The wonderful thing about such variety is that you have the flexibility to find a Bible that suits your reading ability and personal style. Look around and see what suits you. Everybody has a favourite. For example, Pete is not too keen on gimmicky Bibles, and he is rather fond of the New Living Translation and Today's New International Version. He often ends up returning, however, to his trusty New International Version, largely because he is mentally stuck in the 1980s when the NIV was very popular. Ben, however, is harder to please. He likes his New Testament in the New American Standard Version, but his Old Testament in the New International Version.***

So there you have it. From humble beginnings in ancient languages on parchment scrolls to being the biggest-selling book in history. What a journey. And to think, until relatively recently, English Bibles were hard to come by. Nowadays, choosing a Bible is harder than trying to pick a new release at your local DVD store on a Friday night.

*One-tenth of an inch.
**Aussie talk for "good", "honest" or "truthful".

***If you think that's picky, you should see Ben at a restaurant!
– Pete

Chapter 12

CHINESE WHISPERS
How do we know the Bible got to us accurately?

When Pete was a teenager going to a youth group every Friday night, he played a game called "Chinese whispers". He has no idea why it was called Chinese whispers but just assumed it was because people from Xiang Province don't like loud noises.

It worked like this: Everyone sat in a circle, and the chosen person would make up a phrase and whisper it to the person on their left. That person would whisper the phrase to the person on *their* left, and so it would go until the whispered message had travelled around the circle back to the person who made it up in the first place.

The whole point of the game was that as the message went around the circle, people would mishear it and pass on a slightly inaccurate version to the next person, which would be misheard again and again. By the time the round finished, the originator would declare that they sent the message

Michelle ate tuna with a tasty green salad

and the last person in the circle would announce – to guffaws and giggles – that they had received the message

In hell, Kate swooned with a pasty bean ballad.

As an irrelevant aside, this was a frustrating and annoying game because it was never played properly. This was usually the fault of the youth-group comedian* who heard the message, "Ten green bottles standing on the wall", and then deliberately mangled it and passed on, "Vegetarian grasshoppers float mysteriously down the Yangtze River." But the message saboteur was always meticulously tracked and held in scorn for at least a week, to say nothing of the bashing he got when the leaders weren't watching.**

Some people have a "Chinese whispers" opinion of the Bible. They know that biblical writings are a few thousand years old, and they assume that they were passed on from person to person, group to group, generation to generation, language to language, and that over the centuries, mistakes and changes

*Read "idiot".

**Thanks, Pete, for that great little story.
— Ben

Are you being sarcastic, Ben? — Pete

No, no seriously. Your stories about your teenage years are riveting. Was there a point to that story? — Ben

Well, yes actually. Read on, Mr. Impatience! — Pete

(both deliberate and accidental) crept in and the words, sentences and meanings changed, so that what we now read as

Jesus said, "I am the way, the truth and the life"

actually began as

Jesus said, "Would you like fries with that?"

Some people have a "Chinese whispers" opinion of the Bible.

In short, they suggest that the Bible is unreliable and that it has changed over the years both through accidental errors (scribes who had drunk too much sherry copying it out badly) and deliberate intervention (publishers getting creative and saying, "Hey, I don't like this crucifixion ending. It's too *down*. Let's jazz it up a bit . . . Hey! What about we bring Jesus back to life again . . . Yeah!").

Okay, so let's work through these concerns.

In the game Chinese whispers, what you basically have is a chain of people. Each person gets the message and passes it along to the next person in the chain. As the errors (both deliberate and accidental) start to creep in, they too are passed along, and so the errors multiply as they move along the chain, until at the end, the message bears little or no resemblance to the original. More to the point, it's hard to hear a whisper, so the game is actually designed for the mistakes to occur. In fact, if the mistakes *didn't* occur, the game would flop! Imagine the scene:

"I sent the message *This is one small step for man.* What message did you get?"

"The same message! Hilarious!"

The Bible did *not* get to the twenty-first century like that. Let's remember that these holy writings were sacred to the ancient Jews and early Christians. They were treated with great respect and care. Way before laser printers, photocopiers and publishing houses, all copies were handwritten by scribes.

These holy writings were sacred to the ancient Jews and early Christians.

Scribes didn't do this as a hobby in their spare time when they weren't farming vegetables. This was their profession. It was a highly valued and important profession. They went to great lengths and followed meticulous rules to ensure the accuracy of their work.

Scribes had to wash themselves and be in full Jewish dress before beginning to copy a scroll. Only the skin of clean animals, specifically prepared for the task, could be used as the writing surface. Even the ink had a special recipe. Every time the scribes copied a page, they would go back and compare the copy to the original word for word. No word and no letter were written from memory. They counted and checked all the letters on each page. They checked the first word of every line and the middle word of every page. A head scribe checked their work. They wrote in columns of no fewer than forty-eight and no more than sixty lines, each with a breadth of thirty letters. Any mistakes or deviations from the rules, and the page would be destroyed. The seriousness of their task is evident in one rule stating that if a scribe was writing the name of God and at that moment he were spoken to by a king, he was to ignore the king until the scribe had finished writing.

So the copies that came down through the generations were meticulously produced, kind of like a game of Chinese whispers where each person checks and confirms their hearing of the message ten times with everyone else around them and compares it to a written version from further up in the line before they pass it on.

The point is that while today's Bible is now available in many different languages and translations, it has not evolved or changed but has remained true to its origins.

In addition, we can cross-reference our twenty-first century Bible with early translations of biblical writings, like the Septuagint,* the Targums,** the Vulgate*** and the previously mentioned Dead Sea Scrolls.

To go back to our game of Chinese whispers, this is like the person at the end of the chain being able to check and compare his or her own message with the first five people in the chain.

By comparing our modern Old Testament with these early writings, we can see that the Bible has *not* changed in two thousand years. Any historian will tell you that the Bible is historically valid and reliable. In fact, of all the manuscripts and documents that you would read about in any Ancient History course, the Bible is without doubt the most supported, most accurate and most researched on the planet.

So rest assured that when you grab that Bible off your shelf and read it, you are reading from a high quality, totally valid, original historical book, just as accurate now as it was way back then.

> The Bible is a high quality, totally valid, original historical book, just as accurate now as it was back then.

*The Greek translation of the Old Testament made around 250 BC.
**Aramaic translations of the original Hebrew made over one hundred years before Christ was born, also referred to as the Syriac translations.
***A Latin translation of both Old and New Testaments, completed in the fourth century AD.

Chapter 13

BIBSCAPE NAVIGATOR
How do you find your way around the Bible?

We will soon move into part 2 of this book, where we will leave behind all this introductory stuff and get into the Bible itself. Before we do, let's sort out an important question: *How do you find your way around the Bible?*

Let's say you want to tell a friend about something interesting you've just read, so you phone them up and say, "Hey, check out this great passage I've just read in the Bible. It's on page 342, about half way down". Immediately you have a problem. If you don't have the *identical* Bible edition that your friend has, *their* page 342 won't match *your* page 342. So how can you accurately and quickly find any single spot in a Bible, regardless of what language it's in or what version it is?

The solution is that, unlike most other books, we don't go by page numbers at all. Instead, each book of the Bible is broken up into chapters, and within each chapter are numbered verses. You wouldn't number the sentences of an essay or a letter to a friend, and neither did the original authors insert the title of each book and number the chapters and verses. All the titles and numbers were put in later, for your convenience.

It is generally believed that Stephen Langton, who later became the Archbishop of Canterbury, first divided the books of the Bible into chapters in AD 1228. Breaking up each book into identifiable sections certainly helped readers navigate each book more easily. But it wasn't enough. Have a look at Psalm 119 (which goes over eight pages in Pete's NIV), and you will realise that further divisions were still needed. So just over two hundred years later (around AD 1448), Rabbi Nathan divided the chapters of the Old Testament into verses.

The New Testament followed suit when a Parisian book printer, Robert Stephanus, divided it into verses in 1551. Rumour has it that Stephanus completed his task while on a journey between Paris and Lyon, and to be blunt, his verses have come under some criticism for their lack of consistency. Sometimes the verse divisions seem to be almost arbitrary. However, it would be impossible to change them now.

The Geneva Bible, which came out in 1560, was the first full Bible to be printed with chapters and verses throughout. Those chapters and verses have

> Breaking up each book into identifiable sections certainly helped readers navigate each book more easily.

stayed ever since. Other components, like subheadings describing sections within chapters (such as "The Ten Commandments", "Solomon Asks for Wisdom", "Jesus Walks on the Water", "Paul's Defence of His Ministry") as well as footnotes and cross-references were also put in later to allow readers to quickly scan for a particular section or to seek out relevant information.

If you already know how to find a specific Bible verse, thanks for coming, and you might as well move on to the next chapter now. Otherwise, let's establish a simple process to help you to find a specific verse in the Bible. It's pretty simple once you know what it all means. ***So how does it work?*** What do you do when you see 1 Corinthians 15:50–58, Matthew 27:62–28:4 or James 3?

Let's run through an example using Judges 4:21. This means you:

1. Turn to the book of Judges.
2. Find chapter 4 (in the book of Judges).
3. Find verse 21 (in the fourth chapter of the book of Judges). The chapter reference is always to the left of the colon (4:), and the verse reference is always to the right of the colon (:21). Sometimes a full stop is used rather than a colon (Judges 4.21).

So let's have a go. Follow these steps:

Step 1 Go to the table of contents at the front of your Bible. Scan through the sixty-six books until you find Judges (Hint: it's in the Old Testament). See what page Judges starts on.

Step 2 Turn to the page in your Bible where Judges starts.

Step 3 Now you're in the right book. Next, you have to flick forward (past chapters 1, 2 and 3) to chapter 4. Chapter references are usually the big bold numbers that are two or three times bigger than the words. They often look like this:

[1]And so Pete and Ben did write a book about the Bible, and it was good.

You may also find the book and chapter reference written at the top of each page for quick reference.

Step 4* In a loud voice, stand up, click your heels together and yell out, "There's no place like home!"

Step 5 Now you're at the fourth chapter of Judges. Next you have to find verse 21. Verse references are the teeny-weeny superscript numbers that are usually about half the size of the words. They often look like this:

[13]Then the computer crashed. [14]Ben and Pete were sorely distressed as they had not backed up their files recently.

Each chapter starts with verse 1. Scan over verses 1, 2, 3, 4, 5 and so on until you get to the little number 21.

Step 6 Read Judges, chapter 4, verse 21. If you're in the right spot, it should say something along the lines of, "But Jael, Heber's wife, picked up a tent peg and a hammer and went quietly to him while he lay fast asleep, exhausted. She drove the peg through his temple into the ground, and he died." (Hey, don't say we didn't warn you that sometimes the Bible is a violent book!)

Step 7* Stand up and call out, "Eureka, I know how to find Bible verses!"

*Step 7 is also optional.

Five Other Things You Need to Know

Thing you need to know no. 1

When you want to refer to a number of consecutive verses, you write it like this: Romans 8:31–39. This means the book of Romans, chapter 8, verses 31, 32, 33, 34, 35, 36, 37, 38 and 39.

Thing you need to know no. 2

When you want to refer to a number of verses that are bunched together, *and they continue into the next chapter*, you write it like this: James 2:14–3:12. This means in the book of James, you start reading at chapter 2, verse 14 and you keep going through chapter 3 until you get to verse 12.

Thing you need to know no. 3

Most books you've ever read have a standard page-numbering system; they start at page 1 and keep going up until the last page. This is very much like Pete's NIV, in which Genesis (the first book of the Old Testament) starts on page 1, and it goes through to the last page of Revelation (the last book of the New Testament), on page 1950.

A word of warning. Some Bibles have separate page numbers for both the Old and New Testaments. So, for example, in Pete's Good News Bible, the Old Testament runs from page 1 to page 1041, and then you turn the page and instead of Matthew starting on page 1042, it begins on page 1. We mention this only to save you from flapping about in the middle of Joshua in the Old Testament, while complaining that the book of Galatians has disappeared from your Bible!

Thing you need to know no. 4

Some Bibles and related literature use abbreviations to refer to books within the Bible. It saves space. So, for example, Psalms is Ps., Matthew is Matt.,

Ezekiel is Ezek., Romans is Rom., and so on. Different publications will have their own system of doing this, so check the table of contents.

Thing you need to know no. 5

Elephants can't jump. No, seriously, it's true. It has to do with the joints in their legs or something. Of course, this has nothing to do with reading the Bible, but it is a good thing to know nonetheless.

Part 2

THE BIG PICTURE

We've covered a lot of ground so far. And now that you know the where, when, how and who of the Bible, it's time to get into the what. The introductions are over, and it's time to leap into the Bible itself.

In the table of contents at the front of your Bible, the sixty-six books are listed one after another from Genesis through to Revelation. But while the table of contents gives you the *order* of the books as they appear, it fails to give you the overall picture of how they fit together in time and in relation to each other. In fact, it gives something of a false picture. In the next chapter, we'll start looking at the first book of the Bible, Genesis. But as part of your overview of the Bible, here are a few things worth knowing.

The Books of the Bible Are Grouped in Sections

While sticking to a general sense of chronology, the books are not strictly ordered by their date of composition. Rather, they are arranged and grouped in sections according to the type of literature. The writings of the prophets, for example, are grouped in the latter part of the Old Testament. Yet many of these prophets were writing at the same time as the events described in 2 Chronicles and 2 Kings, which appear much earlier in the Bible, as they are grouped with the History Books. The figures on **page 82** show you the order and groupings of the books as they appear in the Bible. You can see, for example, that in the English Bible, all of the historical narratives (in the Old Testament) are grouped together and all of Paul's letters (in the New Testament) are grouped together.

The Books of the Bible Are Grouped Somewhat Arbitrarily

Keep in mind that the books of the Bible were not originally composed in the groups in which they are now listed. The practice of grouping similar literature together under specific categories (Law, Prophets, Letters) was undertaken later so that the overall flow of the Bible maintained a sense of narrative structure. So, for example, in the Old Testament, a distinction is made between the more influential prophets (the Major Prophets) and the less influential (the Minor Prophets).

In the New Testament, the book of Revelation is a letter, yet it is not grouped with the other letters, but on its own, because of its unique style. Similarly, while the books of Matthew, Mark, Luke and John obviously describe historical events, they are not called "History Books" (as is the book of Acts), but rather "Gospels" because of their unique nature.

Grouping and Order of Books in the Old Testament

Law Books	History Books	Wisdom and Poetry Books	Prophetic Books
Genesis	Joshua	Job	Isaiah*
Exodus	Judges	Psalms	Jeremiah*
Leviticus	Ruth	Proverbs	Lamentations*
Numbers	1 Samuel	Ecclesiastes	Ezekiel*
Deuteronomy	2 Samuel	Song of Songs	Daniel*
	1 Kings		Hosea
	2 Kings		Joel
	1 Chronicles		Amos
	2 Chronicles		Obadiah
	Ezra		Jonah
	Nehemiah		Micah
	Esther		Nahum
			Habakkuk
			Zephaniah
			Haggai
			Zechariah
*Major prophets			Malachi

Grouping and Order of Books in the New Testament

History Books	Epistles (Letters)		Revelation
Matthew*	Romans**	Titus**	Revelation
Mark*	1 Corinthians**	Philemon**	
Luke*	2 Corinthians**	Hebrews	
John*	Galatians**	James	
Acts	Ephesians**	1 Peter	
	Philippians**	2 Peter	
	Colossians**	1 John	
	1 Thessalonians**	2 John	
	2 Thessalonians**	3 John	
*Gospels	1 Timothy**	Jude	
**Paul's letters	2 Timothy**		

The Books of the Bible Overlap

Because the books of the Bible are presented one after the other, it's easy to assume that each one follows on from the one before, like train carriages in a long line.

This is not so. The Bible is not like a novel that runs chapter after chapter in a neat lineal progression. There is a lot of overlap. In the Old Testament, the books of Exodus, Leviticus, Numbers and Deuteronomy deal with different aspects of events relating to Moses and the lives of the early Israelites. Similarly, the books of 1 Samuel, 2 Samuel, 1 Kings and 1 Chronicles are all concerned with the life of King David, while many pages later, the books of Psalms and Proverbs relate to the writings and sayings of King David and his son King Solomon. In the New Testament, the books of Matthew, Mark, Luke and John tell of the same time period and events relating to Jesus in four different ways.

The Books of the Bible Come in Many Different Sizes

In the Bible's table of contents, the title of each book occupies one line, almost implying that there is consistency in the size of the books. This is not the case. Have a look at the book of Psalms (the longest book in the Bible), for example, and compare it to the second letter written by John (2 John), which is the shortest book in the Bible. Because different people wrote the books for different audiences and different purposes, there is no consistency in their length.

The Books of the Bible Cover a Range of Time Periods

In most of the books, time passes and historical periods are covered at a fairly constant rate. A history textbook, for example, might cover one century in each chapter. Not so in the Bible. The chart on this page shows that some books cover events lasting hundreds of years, while others are written just for that moment. The book of 2 Chronicles, for example, spans a time period *approximately four times longer* than all the books of the New Testament put together.

Comparison of Time Periods Covered in Books of the Bible

100 years	200 years	300 years	400 years

2 Chronicles 384 years

Judges 335 years

Ezra 81 years

Nehemiah 14 years

Jonah 1 month

New Testament 100 years

The Old Testament Is Longer Than the New Testament

Okay, so this might be a bit obvious, but it is interesting nonetheless. Despite the fact that the Bible is divided into two main sections, they do not represent equal halves of the whole. Not only does the Old Testament have more books than the New Testament, it also has more than its fair share of the longest books.

In total, the Old Testament makes up approximately 77 percent of the Bible, compared to the New Testament's 23 percent. Have a look at the chart below to compare how the various sections of the Bible contribute to its content.

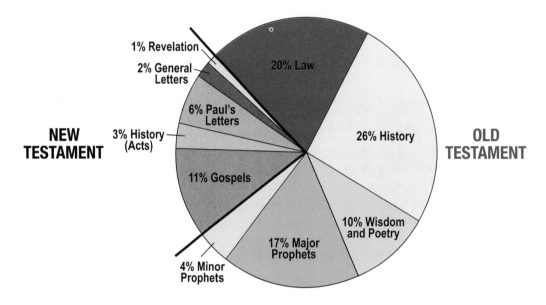

But this should be no surprise. The Old Testament covers a period of history spanning millennia, whereas the New Testament covers the relatively short period of only one century.

The Old Testament

Following the advice of Julie Andrews in *The Sound of Music*, we will "start at the very beginning", as apparently, this is a "very good place to start".

When you read the Bible, you begin with the book of Genesis, chapter 1, verse 1: "In the beginning God created the heavens and the earth."

Along with Schwarzenegger's "I'll be back" and Shakespeare's "To be or not to be", the first sentence of the Bible is one of the most well-known sentences in the world. The Bible begins "at the very beginning" – not just the beginning of the century, or even of the millennium, but the *very* beginning. The beginning of *everything*. The start of it all.

The opening chapters of the book of Genesis describe the creation of the world, tell us who God is and narrate the opening moments of humankind's existence on this rock we call Earth. It was not written as a science textbook. You will not find any references here to interplanetary geophysics, space-time continuums, genetic biology, inflation theory, quarks, mass-to-energy conversions or dinosaurs. In fact, that was far from the author's mind. He was concerned with the *why* and *who* of creation, not the scientific *how*. These opening chapters have a poetic feel about them and were perhaps originally designed to give ancient readers a way of understanding the origin of life in a style similar to other accounts of that time.

In the first two chapters of Genesis, we are immediately introduced to God, without any explanation of his existence. God has always existed. Doesn't need any buildup. He simply *is*. He is *eternal* in that he always has been and always will be. He is *powerful* in that he creates and fashions things simply by saying it is so. He is *distinct* and separate from creation in that he does not rely upon anything to create. He is *unique* in that he is the one and only God, and there are no other gods, except for the fictional creations of humans. He is *holy* and *perfect,* without faults or problems. He is *omnipresent,* in that he is everywhere at once and has a total awareness of his creation. (We could go on and on.) Put simply, God really is . . . **God**.

> The opening chapters of the book of Genesis describe the creation of the world, tell us who God is and narrate the opening moments of humankind's existence on this rock we call Earth.

From time to time, you might hear the opinion that the Earth is a cosmic side effect of a galactic explosion and that living creatures and humans are some kind of chemical accident, the result of a bolt of lightning hitting a puddle of mud. As such, our very existence is, well, a fluke. (Take, for example, the infamous statement attributed to physics and astronomy professor Edward P. Tryon that the universe is just "one of those things which happens from time to time"!)[1] The Bible challenges this viewpoint straight up. God created everything in an orderly and systematic fashion that suggests control, purpose and excellence. He created the heavens and the earth, night and day, land and ocean, vegetation, creatures of the sky and the air and water. He created the farthest star and the hydrogen atom. We don't know all the details, but that's not the point.

> God created everything in an orderly and systematic fashion that suggests control, purpose and excellence.

The final and most important item on God's "Memo to Self: List of Things to Create", and the pinnacle of creation, was the human being. He created a man (named *Adam*) and a woman (named *Eve*). Our ancestors were not like the rest of creation. They had, as we have, the unique privilege of being "created in God's image", not just as a cosmic accident but as a reflection of God's own character. Adam and Eve were given the awesome responsibility to rule over everything else God had made. They were given instructions by God on how to live and were warned about the consequences of disobeying him.

One of the founding fathers of twentieth-century cosmology, the British astrophysicist Sir Fred Hoyle, once said, "There is a coherent plan in the universe, though I don't know what it's a plan for." The Bible, however, tells us exactly what the plan is for. The plan is for God and humankind to be in relationship with each other. It is as simple, and simultaneously as mind-boggling, as that.

Adam and Eve had authority over all creation, but God ultimately ruled them. He was in control, and under his uninterrupted rule, everything was "good". At this point of history, people were in a perfect relationship with God, and all was peachy.

---

[1] E. P. Tryon, "Is the Universe a Vacuum Fluctuation?" *Nature* 246 (1973): 396.

Where are we?

We're in the opening pages of the Bible – the first two chapters of Genesis.

What time is it?

There are different views on the timing of the Earth's creation. Some people take a literal view and say this all took place about six thousand years ago.* They say, for example, that the "seven days" it took to create everything were seven twenty-four-hour days just as we know them. Others take a nonliteral view and suggest that these opening chapters are descriptive rather than scientific. On this understanding, the time frame could be spread over millions of years, a long, long time ago. The seven days of creation could also be just a way of describing a period of time.

In a nutshell

Genesis 1 and 2 describe the ultimate supreme being, God, creating the world and people. God is all-powerful and good. And all that he made was good. God ruled, and humans had a good relationship with him.

Who are the main people?

Adam and Eve

Miscellaneous

- The title *Genesis* means "origin" or "beginning". *Eden* means "delight" or "bliss".

- Genesis is quoted 260 times in the New Testament and, as such, is the third-most-quoted Old Testament book.

- On Christmas day 1968, the *Apollo 8* mission emerged from the dark side of the moon. The story goes that as the three astronauts inside the tiny capsule saw earth rise over the moon's horizon, they read from Genesis to the whole world, "In the beginning, God created the heavens and the earth."

- Sir Fred Hoyle claimed, "The likelihood of the formation of life from inanimate matter is one to a number with 40,000 noughts after it ... It is big enough to bury Darwin and the whole theory of evolution. There was no primeval soup, neither on this planet nor any other ... Once we see, however, that the probability of life originating at random is so utterly minuscule as to make the random concept absurd, it becomes sensible to think that the favourable properties of physics, on which

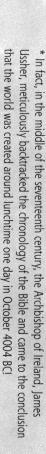

* In fact, in the middle of the seventeenth century, the Archbishop of Ireland, James Ussher, meticulously backtracked the chronology of the Bible and came to the conclusion that the world was created around lunchtime one day in October 4004 BC!

life depends, are in every respect deliberate … It is, therefore, almost inevitable that our own measure of intelligence must reflect higher intelligence – even to the extreme idealized limit of God."[2]

- The first five books of the Bible are commonly referred to as the Pentateuch, meaning "five books". Jews call them the Torah, or Law.

- The Hebrew title of the book of Genesis translates as "In the beginning ".

---

[2] Sir Fred Hoyle and Chandra Wickramasinghe, *Evolution from Space*, (New York: Simon and Schuster, 1984), 148.

Chapter 16

WE STUFF IT UP
The fall, the flood and the building of Babel
Genesis 3-11

A few years ago, Pete and his wife and three young daughters were at a pool party at a mate's place. The sun was shining, the water was cool and there were massive racks of smoking ribs on the barbie.* One of Pete's daughters started pushing the other kids into the water.

Pete scooped his daughter away from the action, sat her down and spoke right into her face. "Okay, listen up. Everyone's enjoying themselves splashing and swimming. This can go on all afternoon. However, there are rules. You are not to push anyone into the pool. Understand? That's dangerous and it's not on. If you push any more kids, I will take you out of the pool and inside the house and that will be the end of it for you. Follow my rules, and everybody's cool. Break my rules, and I will strike like a deadly cobra . . . um, I mean . . . break my rules, and you're out of there. Your choice."

Seventeen seconds later, his daughter was in the house.

This part of Genesis tells of some pretty dark moments in human history. It describes the very beginnings of a great tragedy, the broken relationship between God and humans. Despite all the benefits of having a dandy time with God in the garden of Eden, Adam and Eve decided to break God's rules and do their own thing, much like Pete's daughter. They decided to "become like God" by doing what God explicitly said not to do, namely, eating the fruit of the forbidden tree. God decreed the punishment for disobedience would be that instead of living forever with their Creator, their days on earth would be numbered and their relationship with God would be broken.

The consequences of disobeying God were devastating and immediate. They were out of the pool and into the house! Adam and Eve were cut off from the special and intimate relationship they had with God and were chucked out of the garden.

There is, however, a glimmer of hope. Despite their disobedience, God didn't give up on Adam and Eve (in the same way parents don't give up on their kids). He still cares for humankind and wants the relationship to be good again, and here begins the great theme of the Bible. It's in colour so you can't

> *Hey, my sister had a barbie once! —Ben
>
> No, Ben, this is barbie as in barbeque. —Pete

> The consequences of disobeying God were devastating and immediate.

miss it. *Here begins God's plan to re-establish the original great relationship between God and humankind that is described in chapters 1 and 2 of Genesis.* (This all heads toward Jesus Christ, but that's for later.)

> Sin is serious stuff. It is a capital offense against God, for which there are serious consequences.

The Flood

Sin (which is a technical word for the act of going against God) corrupted the thoughts and actions of people. To many people in our society today, the word *sin* has almost become antiquated religious gobbledygook, which evokes images of naughty children being sent to their bedroom. Not so. Sin is serious stuff. It is a capital offence against God, for which there are serious consequences. The human race multiplied and spread, but so did their rejection of God and their evil ways. People were selfish, corrupt and violent, and eventually it became so bad that God was sorry he had ever created them. He decided to destroy his creation with a flood. However, he found one bloke who was trying to do the right thing.

Noah is described as a "righteous man . . . [who] walked faithfully with God" (Genesis 6:9), meaning that he tried to live a life that was pleasing to God. Here we read one of the most famous stories in the Bible. God graciously saved Noah and his family and a bunch of animals, while the rest of creation was destroyed. It was a chance for humankind to start over with God again.

The City and Tower of Babel

Every so often, we humans achieve some technical, scientific or medical breakthrough that totally raises the bar of human achievement. The splitting of the atom, heart transplants, the mapping of human DNA, genetic engineering, space travel and in vitro fertilization have all been heralded by some blockhead as evidence that humans have taken the place of God. Things weren't that different during the times of Genesis.

After the flood, people again began to populate the earth. But they continued to rebel against God. United in their pride to "make a name" for themselves, they began to build a city and a tower that reached "to the heavens" as a trophy of human endeavour (Genesis 11:4).

God again judged and humbled the human race by scattering them all over the land and confused them by giving them different languages.

Where are we?

Hopefully, you aren't lost yet. We're still near the beginning of the Bible, in its opening book, Genesis.

What time is it?

The stories of these chapters are still a long, long time ago – way before 2000 BC, in a period many people refer to as "prehistory".

In a nutshell

The third chapter of Genesis explains why the world is full of sin. It describes Adam and Eve's rebellion against God's commands and the punishment for doing so. The chapters that follow narrate the ongoing effects of sin and the way God deals with it in the stories of Noah's ark and the building of the city and tower of Babel.

Who are the main people?

Adam and Eve, Cain and Abel (Adam and Eve's sons), Noah and his family.

Miscellaneous

- Contrary to the popular cliché, there is no mention of an "apple" in the Genesis account of the garden. It simply states "fruit".

- Some of the words and concepts found in these early chapters of Genesis are still in common use today:
  - In *Star Trek III*, a "Genesis bomb" goes off, bringing new life to a dead planet.
  - In the *Hitchhiker's Guide to the Galaxy* series, characters insert a "Babel fish" into their ears to translate foreign languages into their own.
  - "Project Ark" is an environmental initiative to save plants and wildlife.
  - Over seventy places in the world are named "Eden".

All great and mighty things started out small. The mightiest river began as a trickle. The tallest tree began as a seed. The fat layer around your stomach began as a creamy jam donut. And at the start of the Bible, we read about the start of something great from a small family.

We read about the birth of a nation – not just any nation, but one that would be special to God. In fact, the rest of the Old Testament from here on in follows the incredible history of this special nation, Israel. It all began with four men, often referred to as patriarchs, "the fathers of Israel".

People who play a critical role in establishing some sort of social movement are often given the title of "father". So, for example, the fathers of science were Copernicus, Galileo, Kepler and Newton. The fathers of rock music were Buddy Holly, Chuck Berry, Sam Phillips and Little Richard. Similarly, the fathers of Israel were Abraham and his son, grandson and great-grandson, respectively, Isaac, Jacob and Joseph. The story of Abraham and his family is the story of the birth of a nation and how God was intent on re-establishing the relationship he wanted with the human race. It is a momentous story, spanning many generations.

Abraham

We are first introduced to Abraham (whose original name was Abram) and his wife Sarah (originally Sarai), in chapter 11 of Genesis. God chose this faithful couple to be the founding parents of a great family, a family that would become a nation and an example of a people in special relationship with God. It is the epic saga of this family, this nation, that we read about when we read the Old Testament. God made a series of promises (called covenants) with Abraham:

- God promised to bless Abraham and his descendants.
- God promised to make Abraham's descendants "as many as the stars".
- God promised that Abraham's family would have a great name and become a great nation.
- God promised that through this nation, the world would be blessed.

- God promised that Abraham and his offspring would be given a place to live and prosper.

In return, God expected his people to be faithful to him and to obey him.

Remember these promises, as they are important to much of the history and activity that follows for the next few hundred years. As you read the rest of the Old Testament, these promises will come up again and again.

All these promises came as a shock to Abraham and his wife because, aside from the fact that Abraham was old and probably gearing up for retirement, Sarah had been unable to conceive children. The idea of being parents of a nation seemed ludicrous! But God was in control, and his plan to save humankind through this family was going to happen no matter what. The first miracle birth of the Bible occurred in Genesis 21 when Sarah gave birth to a son, Isaac.

Abraham and Isaac

Abraham's faith in God was soon tested when he was told to offer his son as a sacrifice to God. In short, God required Abraham to give him his most precious and special "possession", his own flesh and blood, his son. To be frank about it, the idea of killing your own child does not sit at all well with us in the twenty-first century. It is an idea that seems cruel, inhuman and barbaric and makes the hairs stand up on the back of your neck. Yet at the same time, it shows that God wants and demands our total and unfailing devotion.

One can only imagine what Abraham must have been thinking at this point. Yet amazingly, he obeyed and took his son up a mountain to kill him.* Isaac, then a boy, asked his father where the animal to be sacrificed was. Abraham replied, "The Lord will provide". These words turned out to be prophetic and at the moment when Abraham was about to kill Isaac, God stopped him and provided an animal to be sacrificed in the boy's place.

Isaac

Isaac grew up and married Rebekah who, like her mother-in-law, also had not been able to have children. But with God's blessing, she miraculously gave birth to twins – Jacob and Esau.

Jacob (a.k.a. Israel)

Jacob must have been a remarkable man. He was the father of twelve sons – born to four different women!** His family story reads like the script of a soap opera.

Jacob was married to the sisters Leah and Rachel. Leah bore Jacob four boys – Reuben, Simeon, Levi and Judah. Because Rachel couldn't have children, she became jealous and gave Jacob her maid Bilhah, to have children on

*The author of Hebrews comments on Abraham's faith in this act, telling us that Abraham believed that God was able to bring his son back from the dead (Hebrews 11:17–19).
**In ancient biblical times, it was quite common for a man to have more than one wife at the same time.

her behalf. Bilhah gave birth to Dan and Naphtali. Then because Leah hadn't had any children in a while, she got jealous and gave Jacob *her* maid Zilpah to have children on *her* behalf. Zilpah gave birth to Gad and Asher. You can imagine old Jacob's head spinning with all this activity. It got worse when Leah started having children again, giving birth to Issachar and some time later, Zebulun, and then a daughter, Dinah. To make things more complicated, Rachel then got pregnant and gave birth to Joseph. A long while later, she died giving birth to Jacob's twelfth son, Benjamin.

God gave Jacob the name Israel. It would be Jacob/Israel's twelve sons who would go on to be the backbone of God's special nation. They would all be the children of Israel, the "Israelites".

In time, the sons each had their own large families, and generation after generation grew to become the twelve great tribes of Israel. When you read the Old Testament, you are reading about the descendants of these brothers.

Of Jacob's twelve sons, Joseph had a special role to play. The remaining chapters of Genesis follow his wild adventures. If you've ever had a younger brother or sister who at some time you wanted to throttle, you might have some insight into the relationship between Joseph and his older brothers. As a seventeen-year-old, Joseph "brought a bad report" about his brothers to their father. (In modern terms, he dobbed* on them for mucking around when they were supposed to be tending the flocks.) This got their backs up, and it just got worse from there. Joseph had vivid dreams and (in an incredible display of poor judgment) told his brothers about dreams he had in which they were bowing down to him and he was their ruler. You can imagine how this presumptuous whippersnapper annoyed his older brothers.

Around the same time, Jacob rubbed salt into the proverbial wound when he presented Joseph with a beautiful coat, displaying his favouritism toward him. His older brothers were incensed with jealousy, so much so, that when they were out with the flocks one day, they faked Joseph's death and sold him to Midianite slavers, who promptly took him off and sold him in Egypt as a servant to Potiphar, one of Pharaoh's officials.

After spending some time in a prison cell in Egypt on a false charge, Joseph's ability to interpret dreams came in handy. Through a series of circumstances, he was brought before the most powerful man in the world at that time, the pharaoh of Egypt, and asked to interpret Pharaoh's troubling dreams. Joseph did so and Pharaoh was so pleased that he made Joseph his right-hand man and gave him a place of great authority in the kingdom.

A few years later, a huge famine caused the rest of Joseph's family to come to Egypt. They sorted out their differences, were reunited and continued to live in prosperity in Egypt, where ironically Joseph was indeed their ruler. By then, the brothers had married and had their own children. Their extended family numbered sixty-eight direct descendants of Jacob, plus wives and children.

> God gave Jacob the name Israel. It would be Jacob/Israel's twelve sons who would go on to be the backbone of God's special nation. They would all be the children of Israel, the "Israelites".

*Aussie talk for "tittle-tattled".

At this stage, things were going pretty well for Jacob and his twelve sons and their families. Some of the promises God had made to Jacob's grandfather were beginning to come true. They were prosperous and on their way to being a huge family dynasty, and Joseph was one of the most powerful and influential men alive.

Where are we?

We're at the end of the first book of the Bible, but don't fret. We'll be moving more quickly in the next chapters.

What time is it?

The lives of Abraham, Isaac, Jacob and Joseph cover a period of almost three hundred years, finishing somewhere around 1800 BC.

In a nutshell

These chapters narrate the stories of four men who were the founding fathers of the nation of Israel. God used each of these men of faith to begin his great plan to save humankind.

Who are the main people?

Abraham, Sarah, Isaac, Rebekah, Jacob, Esau, Leah, Rachel, Joseph and his eleven brothers, Potiphar (Joseph's master), Pharaoh (the ruler of Egypt).

Miscellaneous

- Abraham became such an example of faith that he is mentioned over seventy times in the New Testament. His name means "father of many".

- Andrew Lloyd Webber made the story of Joseph into a musical called *Joseph and the Technicolor Dreamcoat.* Interestingly, the Bible does not say it was colourful, merely that it was a "richly ornamented robe".

- It is likely that Joseph and his family were in Egypt in an era when it was under the rule, not of a native Egyptian, but of a foreign invader Hyksos king.

- Joseph was sold to slavers for twenty shekels of silver.

- The twelve tribes of Israel each took their name from their founding father, Levi's family became the Levites, Reubenites were descendants of Reuben, and so on.

At the end of Genesis, the twelve tribes (or great families) of Israel had survived the vast famine, moved to Egypt and been reunited with their "lost" brother Joseph.

Some time later, Jacob (the father of the twelve sons) died. In time, Joseph also died, departing with a promise to his brothers that God would take them back to the land he had promised their great-grandfather. That sounded quite good. But a year went by. Then another. Then ten. Twenty. Fifty. One hundred.

In fact, four hundred years later (when the book of Exodus kicks off), their descendants were still in Egypt, but life was a different story. All memories and good feelings toward Jacob's family and the great leader Joseph had long been forgotten. The descendants of the twelve tribes had become so numerous that the Egyptian pharaoh considered them a potential political and military threat. He imposed harsh slavery on the Israelites and used them to build the Egyptian cities of Pithom and Rameses.

The promises made to Abraham hundreds of years earlier about Israel becoming a great nation and having their own land must have seemed dark and distant. All seemed lost. But God chose a special leader to rescue his people and bring them out of slavery. The name of the deliverer was . . . fanfare trumpet, maestro! . . . Moses.

Everyone has heard of Moses. The very name conjures up images of Charlton Heston with a huge beard being pursued by Yul Brynner across the desert in Cecil B. DeMille's movie *The Ten Commandments*, complete with 219 minutes of dazzling circa-1956 special effects. Or perhaps for modern audiences, it is more the Val Kilmer – voiced young spunk Moses from the Dreamworks cartoon *Prince of Egypt*.

Moses was saved from death as a baby and raised in the royal family of Egypt. He was given a special mission by God to go before Pharaoh and plead for the release of his people. But Pharaoh's heart was hard toward God. Pharaoh was not keen to let his massive slave workforce just waltz out of town. So he refused.

There was a standoff. "Aaaaaaaaand in the left corner, weighing in at 85 kilos,* is Phayrooooh, ruler of Egypt, refyuuusing to free the Israelite slaves.

* 187 pounds.

Aaaaaaaaand in the right corner, weighing in at several billion kilos and ruler of . . . well, pret-ty-well-ev-er-y-thing . . . is the Loooord, who wants Pharaoh to let his people go."

In a tremendous display of power, God was going to make it clear to Pharaoh that he could no longer unjustly enslave the Israelites. Pharaoh was a bit slow to catch on, so God hit Egypt with a series of plagues. It must have been like living in a nightmare. The Nile River turned to blood, and there were infestations of frogs, gnats and flies. All the livestock died. The citizens were covered in hideous weeping boils, and their houses were smashed by hail. Locusts swept across the land, and darkness was everywhere.*

But God kept the worst plague until last. It was a plague that would bring Egypt and Pharaoh to their knees. On one particular night, the firstborn son of each family was to die. To avoid the curse of sudden death, God instructed the Israelites to smear the door frames of their houses with the blood of a sacrificial lamb or goat. They were to roast the meat over a fire and eat it along with bitter herbs and bread. He promised to "pass over" all those houses marked with this sign of blood, and the children would be spared. It was such a significant moment in Israel's history that they were instructed to remember God's mighty rescue each year in the **Feast of the Passover.****

At midnight, God struck down the oldest child in each family throughout Egypt. Imagine the hysteria and sorrow that must have followed. The death of the oldest child in each family, probably including Pharaoh's own, proved to be the final straw for the ruler. He finally realised that he had bitten off more than he could chew in trying to stand against God. He surrendered and permitted Jacob's descendants to leave the country.

Many years ago, Ben and Pete travelled overseas to play at a big youth music festival. There were four rock bands in their touring party. The logistics of organizing the travel arrangements were nightmarish. The managers had to organise transport to and from airports for this large group, plus air tickets, accommodation and food. On top of that, each band had mountains of luggage, largely made up of guitar-effects racks and hair gel. It was a massive undertaking trying to get this mass of rockers from point A to point B. Imagine how much bigger it was for Moses!

Moses led over 600,000 Israelites out of Egypt. You can imagine the excitement as they literally packed up and walked out to freedom. After four hundred years, they were finally returning to their own land. This event was big. *Really* big. Three months and three hundred kilometres*** later, the Israelites set up camp at the foot of Mount Sinai. They were a free people, and the promise made to Abraham (and reiterated to Isaac, Jacob and Joseph) of having their own land at last looked like it would come to pass.

*Take note: when God wants to prove a point, he does not muck around.
**This annual celebration was still going on fifteen hundred years later during New Testament times (and in fact, it is still celebrated today), but more of that later.
***186 miles.

After four hundred years of being told what to do, there might have been a sense among the people of, "Well, what now? Who are we? What do we do? Huh? How do we live? Anyone . . . any ideas? Huh? Huh?"

Moses went up the mountain to meet with God. He was probably thinking, "Okay God, you've got us this far. Now what?" God gave Moses a very important message for the people. At the historic start of their new society, he laid it all out on the table. God said that if they obeyed him fully and kept his covenant, they would be his special "treasured possession" and a "holy nation" above all the other nations. He went on to give the people a set of laws to live by, known as the Ten Commandments.* These commandments were to be used as the basis for the Israelites' conduct and the foundation for their society. Moses was also given complicated details relating to worship and instructions on the building of a special place (called the tabernacle – more about that in the next chapter) where God and his people could meet together.

The Ten Commandments began with God telling Moses and the Israelites, "I am the LORD your God, who brought you out of Egypt, out of the land of slavery" (Exodus 20:2). This statement was the governing thought for the entire principle behind the law. The sequence of events is important. The law was given to the Israelites *after* they have been freed from slavery. God had already rescued the people. Obeying the law was not the *means* of the people getting delivered by God, but the *response* to it.

There were, in fact, 613 specific commands given to Moses. These are most clearly expressed in **the Ten Commandments,** which were:

- Don't have other gods.
- Don't make and worship idols.
- Don't use God's name badly.
- Remember the Sabbath (seventh) day, and rest on that day.
- Honour your father and mother.
- Don't murder.
- Be faithful to your spouse.
- Don't steal.
- Don't tell lies.
- Don't be jealous of what others have.

These laws formed the basis of Israelite society and would in time be responsible for the legal and ethical code that we live under today.

If you've seen the Dreamworks cartoon *Prince of Egypt*, this is the part where the story finishes. Moses triumphantly comes down from the mountain as the people of Israel wait expectantly below. Cue music. Roll credits.

What a pity the cartoon didn't show you what happened next!

Moses walked back into camp to find that the Israelites had got impatient waiting for him to return. They had melted down all their jewellery and created

Obeying the law was not the *means* of the people getting delivered by God, but the *response* to it.

an idol (a gold calf) to worship. Moses arrived to find a bit of a party going on, with drinking, dancing and general sexual activity. He went berserk when he found they had so quickly taken on the practices of the surrounding ungodly nations, when they were supposed to be faithful. He ground the gold calf into powder and made the people drink it, and about three thousand people were killed in punishment for what they had done.* In addition, God declared that none of them would actually make it to the Promised Land. They would all die, and it would be their children who would get to the land.**

Unfortunately, this was just the first of many similar problems for Israel. Unfaithfulness and idolatry would plague Israel for many years to come, as time and time again they rejected God and adopted the immoral practices and beliefs of pagan nations.

These are just the opening moments of the epic saga to follow. Israel had an incredible roller-coaster ride and years of ups and downs, adventures and disasters, ahead of them.

Where are we?

The story of the exodus starts in the book of Exodus chapter 1 and finishes when Moses and the Israelites come to Mount Sinai and are given the law, in chapter 20.

What time is it?

Exodus chapter 1 provides a quick jump over the 350 years from the arrival of Jacob in Egypt (around 1875 BC), picking up the narrative again many years later with the new pharaoh, who did not know Joseph. The rest of the book covers an eighty-year period, beginning with Moses's birth in 1525 BC and finishing with the construction of the tabernacle.

In a nutshell

After hundreds of years of slavery in a foreign land, God raised up Moses, sent plagues on the Egyptians and then led Israel through the Red Sea to Mount Sinai, where they were given the law.

Who are the main people?

Moses, Aaron and Miriam (Moses's brother and sister), Pharaoh.

Miscellaneous

- As a role model to all senior citizens, Moses was eighty years old when he led the Israelites out of Egypt (not a handsome thirtysomething, as the *Prince of Egypt* cartoon would have you believe).

- The name *Exodus* means "departure" or "exit".

- The Red Sea is actually a "Sea of Reeds", a freshwater lake.

- Exodus is quoted 250 times in the New Testament and, as such, is the fourth-most-quoted Old Testament book.

- Moses is the third-most-mentioned person in the Bible (740 times), behind Jesus and King David.

- The Feast of the Passover is still a very important event celebrated in Jewish communities today.

Chapter 19

GOD'S GREAT TENT
The tabernacle
Exodus 25-40, Leviticus

Remember back to the book of Genesis? After a good start, humans disobeyed God, and their relationship with him was damaged.

The good news of the Bible, however, is that God still loves us and wants to restore the broken relationship and "dwell" with us again. He wants to get to how things were supposed to be in the first place. But there is a problem. God is holy and cannot tolerate sin. Humans are sinful. These are two opposites that can't be brought together. *What to do?*

The book of Exodus describes how God instructed Moses and the Israelites to build a portable sanctuary (which means "holy place"), where sin would be dealt with on a regular basis and where God could be with his people again.

This **tabernacle** (which means "dwelling place") was not a marble palace, nor a stately mansion, but a two-room tent. Pete and his family also have a two-room tent. It's a big canvas beast with steel poles; it weighs a tonne and smells of mothballs. They use the outer room for cooking and playing cards and an inner chamber for sleeping and escaping mosquitoes. But the Downey family tent is nothing compared to the tabernacle. The tabernacle was a serious tent. It was big, sturdy and made out of the finest materials by the best craftsmen – finely twisted linen and yarn, bronze clasps, goat hair and ram skin supported by acacia wood poles overlaid with gold and mounted in silver bases. It would be the pride of any modern campground.

The tabernacle sat in a fenced rectangular courtyard about the size of an Olympic swimming pool. Inside the courtyard were a basin for washing and a bronze altar for sacrifices. At the far end, the tabernacle was 13.6 metres long by 4.5 metres wide.* There were no windows and just one entrance. The first room and entrance was the Holy Place. The second room, separated by a thick woven curtain and in the shape of a cube, was the Most Holy Place. (Not the most creative names, but there you have it.)

In the Holy Place was an acacia wood table overlaid with gold, a pure gold lampstand and altar, where incense was burned. It was certainly more elaborate than the Downey's tent with its low laminex table, hurricane gas lamp and mosquito coils.

> God instructed Moses and the Israelites to build a portable sanctuary, where sin would be dealt with on a regular basis and where God could be with his people again.

*About 15 yards by 5 yards.

But the Most Holy Place was where the action really was. Do you remember Indiana Jones' quest in the movie *Raiders of the Lost Ark*? Well, the Most Holy Place was where that ark ("the ark of the covenant") first resided. It was an acacia wood chest, overlaid and elaborately decorated with gold, and was home to the two stone tablets on which the Ten Commandments were written. The ark was extremely special and valuable to the Israelites. In fact, while only the priests could go into the Holy Place, only the chief priest could go into the Most Holy Place, and even he went in only once a year.

When the tabernacle was finally completed, the Spirit of God rested, or "dwelt", above the ark in the Most Holy Place. Here at last, for the first time since Adam and Eve were cast out of the garden, God and humans were dwelling together again, even though the relationship was limited. God's tent was pitched right in the midst of the Israelites' camp. He chose the Levites (descendants of the family of Levi) to be the priests who would carry and maintain the tabernacle and perform the sacrifices in it. Hence, the book of Leviticus was written primarily to the Levites as an instruction manual about when and how they were to perform their duties as priests.

Here at the tabernacle, and later at the temple, was where sacrifices took place.

Sacrifices, did you say!?

Yes, sacrifices. Let us explain. But first, get the image out of your head of crazed Indiana Jones voodoo men with grotesque masks and buffalo horns, slaughtering unwilling peasants on some mountaintop altar surrounded by flames.

God took his relationship with humankind very seriously. And the one thing that didn't go down well was sin. In the same way that parents teach their children that their actions and attitudes have consequences, God made it clear that disobedience would be punished. The punishment for sin isn't just a slap on the wrist or being sent to your room without any dessert. The punishment for disobeying God is death.

Yet out of love for his people, God provided a temporary way out of this punishment by initiating the sacrificial system. God determined that a substitute could die in the place of the sinful person or persons. In this way, the substitute would symbolically receive the punishment on behalf of the guilty, and the one who really deserved to be punished was saved from God's wrath. So throughout the Old Testament, you often read about people offering sacrifices to God, in the form of birds, sheep, oxen and so on. These were offered to God not because he was morbid or bloodthirsty but as an acknowledgment that sin was serious and needed to be dealt with.

Israel camped around the tabernacle and brought certain animals to the priests for sacrificing. In this way, the punishment for their sin could be dealt with temporarily. All this sacrificing of animals was a messy business. Animals

> God took his relationship with humankind very seriously. And the one thing that didn't go down well was sin.

were cut open, their blood was shed on the altar and what remained of their corpses was completely burned. This may seem cruel, and it doesn't sit well with our twenty-first-century values. It's pretty gross and smelly and disgusting. In fact, if you went to church today and halfway through the service the minister went up to the communion table and slit the throat of a goat, half the congregation would faint, and the other half would need counselling for many months afterward. The sacrifices, however, served as a great reminder that breaking God's commands is very serious and that sin means death and separation from God's blessings.

All of this was just the beginning. Ultimately, God would deal with our sin once and for all with an almighty sacrifice, and as a result, he would fully dwell with us as he did in the beginning. But more of that later.

Where are we?

We have now completed the first three books of the Bible. The instructions for building and using the tabernacle were given to Moses in the final chapters of Exodus. The book following, Leviticus, contains the instructions given to the priests from the tribe of Levi.

What time is it?

The tabernacle was built soon after Moses received the commandments. That means it was probably constructed around 1445 BC.

In a nutshell

The tabernacle was the portable sanctuary that God instructed Israel to build. Once built, it was used as the place where sin could be dealt with and the place where God would dwell with his people.

Who are the main people?

Moses, Aaron, the tribe of Levi.

Miscellaneous

- The tabernacle was set up in such a way that its one and only entrance faced east (just like the garden of Eden). That meant that to enter it, one walked in facing west. In Genesis 3–11, the direction of east symbolised walking *away* from God. Here, walking westward symbolised a turning away from sin and walking *toward* God.

- Jewish folklore suggests that when the high priest went through the curtain into the Most Holy Place, a rope was tied around him so if he died while in there, the others could drag him out without having to enter.

- Some of the instructions in Leviticus were universal laws, like Don't be a gossip, Show respect for older people, Don't have sex with another man's wife and Do not make fun of the deaf. Others, however, were more cultural and can be a bit confusing to the modern reader, like being forbidden to shave any part of your head, not being allowed to eat pigs or rabbits, considering a woman unclean for up to sixty-six days after childbirth and having to burn clothes that have mildew spots on them.

Have you ever been generous to someone, only to have your generosity thrown back in your face with rudeness and ingratitude?

One night when Pete was ten years old, his mother rushed home from work, as she always did, to cook the evening meal. She served up stew with beans and carrots and potatoes. Pete came in from twilight street tennis, sat down at the table and scowled at the meal. With the egocentric lack of awareness common to his age, he complained to his mother that she never served up good things like hamburgers and chips and fizzy drink, and he topped it off by saying that he was sick of boring meals like stew and spuds.

Showing remarkable self-control, Pete's mum took a deep breath, paused, quietly removed his meal and sent him to his room without any dinner. It was a valuable lesson. It was the last time Pete ever took his mother (and her cooking) for granted. It is frustrating and hurtful when you do something good for someone and they metaphorically spit in your face. (It's even worse if they *literally* spit in your face.) Unfortunately, this is the kind of treatment God got from the Israelites. He had rescued them from slavery in Egypt, given them rules to live by and promised them land to call their own. When the Israelites walked out of Egypt, they were homeless. God promised to provide a home for them in Canaan, a place they referred to as "the Promised Land". It was the strip of land we now call Palestine. The Bible describes it as being "fertile", "good" and the place of God's blessing.

Everything looked set for the promises made to Abraham to be fulfilled. The Israelites spent a year near Mount Sinai, building the tabernacle and preparing for their journey. This was to be no simple afternoon stroll, but a large-scale march of military proportion.

They packed up their camp to make their journey to the land, a journey that should have taken less than two weeks. Things didn't go as planned, however.

You would imagine that following the golden-calf incident, the Israelites would have had their proverbial tails between their legs and treated God with more respect. If anything, they did the opposite. The people complained and wailed and whined every step of the way about the food and

> Everything looked set for the promises made to Abraham to be fulfilled.

the harsh conditions. They grumbled about how life was better in Egypt. They trembled in fear when their scouts discovered the land of Canaan was occupied by strong people with fortified cities. They even planned a rebellion and plotted to kill Moses and Aaron and head back to Egypt, where life now seemed easier.

God was not happy. He was not happy with their grumbling, their lack of faith and their disrespect. He called them wicked and stiff-necked, and as punishment for their contempt, he declared that none of them would live in the Promised Land. They would all die in the desert, and it would be their children who would occupy the new land.

So they wandered from place to place in the desert for decades.* Almost forty years passed after the family of Israel left Egypt, and by then, a new generation stood before Moses on the border of Canaan. The book of Deuteronomy records Moses' final words to this new generation of Israelites as they gathered on the plains of Moab. Under these circumstances, through Moses' three speeches, God renewed his promises and reminded his people to keep his commandments, or they would lose his blessing and the land they were about to receive. Like the books before it, Deuteronomy shows us that God is in control, working to fulfil his promises and restore the relationship that man had broken. The love between God and his people and the call to total commitment through obedience and worship are themes that pervade the whole book.

Just when the family of Israel was preparing to go into the Promised Land, their great leader Moses died. God chose Joshua, Moses' helper, for the job of leading Israel into Canaan. The book of Joshua thus begins with this transition of leadership.

One of the first things God told Joshua was that the Israelites were to cross the Jordan River and take the land he was giving them. The circumstances were not going to be easy however. Jacob and his family had been in Egypt for hundreds of years, and the Promised Land had been occupied by peoples from various surrounding nations. It wasn't a case of just turning up and saying, "Right, sorry everyone, but this is our land. We've just been stuck in Egypt. But guess what? We're here now, so if you could all toddle off, that would be great." Nothing as easy as that. They were going to have to fight for the land. Under these circumstances, God told Joshua and the Israelites to be "strong and courageous" and to "be careful to obey" all his commandments.

The first five chapters of the book of Joshua record the spiritual, moral, physical and military preparations of Israel before they began their conquest of the Promised Land. Then come some of the most fascinating and violent chapters of the Bible, as they describe Israel's dramatic entrance into the

God renewed his promises and reminded his people to keep his commandments, or they would lose his blessing and the land they were about to recieve.

Promised Land through the Jordan River and the battles that followed. Here we read of some pretty ferocious encounters as the Israelites fought and conquered their opponents.

The Israelites, however, went against God's advice and failed to completely eliminate their adversaries, allowing some of them to stay. (This would turn out to be a mistake that had serious consequences.) Once the family of Israel took control of the land, it was divided among the twelve tribes. The book of Joshua concludes with Joshua giving a moving sermon in which he reviews God's gracious actions and encourages the Israelites to remain faithful to God. Joshua died, and we read that the Israelites who outlived him continued to serve God in their new land.

Where are we?

The books of Numbers and Deuteronomy conclude the Pentateuch (the first five books of the Bible). Joshua is the sixth book of the Bible and is the first of the twelve History Books of the Old Testament. It details Israel's history leading up to the book of Judges.

What time is it?

Following Moses' receiving the Ten Commandments and a year of preparation, Numbers spans thirty-eight years of the life of Israel as they wander to the Promised Land. Deuteronomy covers a short period of about one month. Moses dies at the end of this book, around the year 1405 BC. The book of Joshua covers a period of about fifteen years.

In a nutshell

Numbers records the story of Israel's journey from Mount Sinai to the plains of Moab, a journey that took almost forty years. Deuteronomy records three of Moses' speeches to Israel on the plains of Moab as they were about to enter the Promised Land. The book of Joshua picks up where Deuteronomy leaves off. It describes the leadership change from Moses to Joshua and the military campaigns of Israel as they conquered more than thirty enemy armies. The book also records the division of the land among the tribes and Joshua's final address to the new nation.

Who are the main people?

Moses and Joshua, Aaron and Miriam.

Miscellaneous

- The name Joshua means "salvation" or "saviour" and is the Hebrew equivalent of the name "Jesus".

- The Hebrew title of the book of Numbers translates as "In the Desert".

- The Hebrew title of the book of Deuteronomy translates as "Words". This title reflects Moses' repetition of the law.

Chapter 21

HERE COME DA JUDGE!
The rule of the judges
Judges, Ruth

If you are expecting the book of Judges to be about hawk-faced men in white wigs and black gowns, sitting behind high oak benches, banging gavels and saying, "It is the decision of this court that you are to be transported to the outer colonies, where you are to spend the term of your natural life", you will be sorely disappointed.

Judges is much more lively than that, as you will quickly discover when you read it. The judges were not like the judges we think of in the modern legal and judicial sense. In fact, they were less like Judge Judy and more like Judge Dredd. When Ben was a kid, one of his favourite comics was Judge Dredd. The judges of this futuristic series roamed the streets on massive motorbikes, fighting crime, protecting those in need and doling out rough justice to bad guys on the spot. They stood up for what is right and weren't afraid of a fight. They appeared whenever bad stuff was going down, much like the judges we read about in the Bible.

The judges were leaders who rescued Israel from the oppression of neighbouring powers. They were men, and one woman, whom God chose and raised up to govern Israel on his behalf. There was no income attached to their office, and they bore no external marks of dignity, but they had a huge impact on the political and religious life of Israel over three centuries.

The book tells of thirteen judges in total. Some, like Deborah, Gideon and Samson, are described in great detail. Others, like Ibzan, Elon and Abdon, are mentioned only in passing. Some, like Tola and Jair, led Israel in times of relative peace, while others, like Ehud, Jephthah and Othniel, were skilled and competent warriors who experienced battle and warfare firsthand.

You will recall that after many years and struggles and adventures, God's people finally claimed those promises made to Abraham. Joshua and the Israelites occupied the land promised to Israel. But after Joshua's generation died, the Israelites forgot about God and all he had done for them. In total disobedience to God's commands, they began to follow and worship the various gods and idols of their neighbours, the Canaanites, Hittites, Amorites, Perizzites, Stalactites and Stalagmites – the very people they failed to drive out of this land as God had commanded them.

> The judges were men, and one woman, whom God chose and raised up to govern Israel on his behalf.

The Israelites adopted the practises of worshiping local fertility gods. Baal and Ashtoreth – two of the most popular gods in the land – were bad news and into stuff like prostitution in their temples and even child sacrifice. As you can imagine, God was not happy that his chosen people had turned their backs on him, had so flagrantly broken his laws and were getting into a whole bunch of nasty stuff.

By now you're probably getting a sense of *déjà vu* about the Israelites' behaviour. God kept doing miraculous things, and instead of gratitude and obedience, his special people kept forgetting about him. Well, get used to it, because it is a continual theme throughout the history of the Old Testament. (And to be honest, it's a continual theme in modern life as well.)

At what should have been one of its greatest moments, Israelite society fell into a time of despair and disorganisation. They were plundered by raiders and were distraught. It happened over and over again. In fact, the entire book of Judges is made up of recurring cycles.

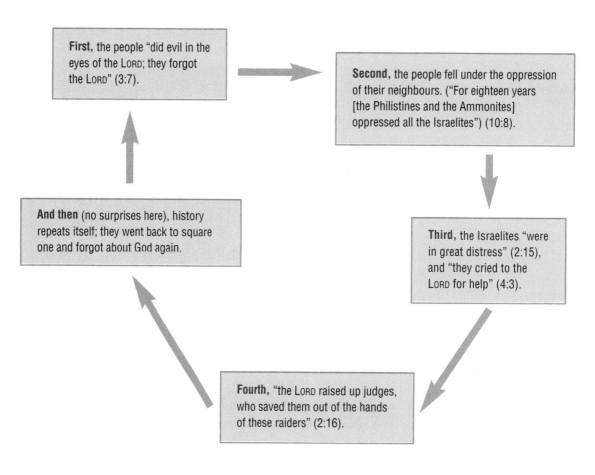

All quotations are from the book of Judges.

So, for example, the Israelites were oppressed for eight years by the king of Aram Naharaim, then saved and led by Judge Othniel for forty years, then oppressed by King Eglon for eighteen years, then saved and led by Judges Ehud and Shamgar for eighty years, then oppressed by the Canaanite King Jabin for twenty years, then saved and led by Judge Deborah for forty years, and on and on it went.

Be warned! The lives and times of the judges are not for the fainthearted. Within moments of the opening of the book, Israel is in battle, and they kill ten thousand men. The violence continued in battle after battle. And there are lots of horror stories. Adoni-Bezek had his thumbs and big toes cut off. Ehud killed King Eglon of Moab by burying a sword up to its hilt in Eglon's obese stomach. The woman Jael killed the Canaanite military commander Sisera by hammering a tent peg through his forehead and into the ground while he lay asleep. The exceptionally strong Samson destroyed a building, killing thousands.

Through the period of the judges, we learn that God is serious about saving his people. He did not like it when they strayed from him to live under foreign leaders. And despite their constant rebellion and sin, God is still in control and is still willing to persevere with his people.

In contrast to Israel's lack of faith and disobedience, the book of Ruth tells the story of Ruth, a foreign woman, and her devotion to God and the people of Israel. A beautiful and popular story set in the time of the judges, it shows how this young Moabite woman devoted herself to the care of her mother-in-law (Ruth 1:16–17) and was richly blessed. The Israelites and the pagan Moabites did not get on well together. It is an example of great benevolence, therefore, that Ruth finds such favour with the Israelites.

The final twist in the narrative is delivered in the last words of the book. Because of her devotion, this destitute widow in a foreign land married the kind and wealthy Israelite, Boaz, and they started a family. We then discover that Ruth would become the great-grandmother of a boy who would grow up to be the greatest ruler in the history of Israel. His name? King David.

> Through the period of the judges, we learn that God is serious about saving his people.

Where are we?

Judges is the second of the History Books of the Old Testament. It takes up where the book of Joshua leaves off and is followed by the book of Ruth, which tells of a faithful woman living during the rebellious era of the judges. After this, the History Books detail the era of the Israelite monarchy.

What time is it?

The events covered in the book of Judges span a period of 335 years, from 1380 BC to 1045 BC. Historically, it narrates the roller-coaster political and religious life of Israel and her surrounding nations after the generation of Joshua but before the rise of the great Israelite kings.

In a nutshell

Judges is about Israel's fluctuating devotion to God and God's faithfulness in rescuing them. The book is made up of several cycles. In short: the Israelites abandon God, are oppressed at the hands of foreign rulers, cry out in distress and are then rescued through the leadership of a judge sent by God. Ruth, in contrast, explores the faithfulness of a Moabite woman to God and her Israelite family.

Who are the main people?

The main judges Othniel, Ehud, Deborah, Gideon, Jephthah and Samson, and the minor judges Shamgar, Tola, Jair, Ibzan, Elon and Abdon. Ruth, Naomi (Ruth's mother-in-law), Boaz (Ruth's new husband).

Miscellaneous

- Judges is one of the most violent books of the Bible.

- Judge Ehud gets one of the most unique descriptions in the Bible. He is "Ehud, a left-handed man" (3:15).

- Cushan-Rishathaim is the second-longest name in the Bible, mentioned in Judges 3:8.

- Ruth is one of only two books in the Bible to bear the name of a woman.

- Ruth is mentioned in the genealogy in the book of Matthew (Matthew 1:5) as being an ancestor of Jesus.

Starring George Clooney, Mark Wahlberg and Ice Cube, the 1999 film *Three Kings* tells the story of three American soldiers of fortune who stumble across a cache of gold during a tour of duty in the Gulf War.

Three thousand years before Clooney and Company were swanning around the Gulf, however, there were three *real* kings, the first kings of Israel. Under the kingship of Saul, David and Solomon, Israel prospered and reached its golden age. Israel was finally a nation with land, a king, military success, economic growth, national security and a temple like nothing the world had ever seen. Some of God's promises had finally come to pass.

The thirteen judges had ruled over Israel for 335 years. When the last judge, Samuel, was getting old, the Israelites pressed him to appoint a king because they wanted to be like other nations. Samuel warned them that if they chose their own king, he would place demands on them, but the Israelites insisted all the same.

> Some of God's promises had finally come to pass.

Saul

So in 1050 BC, Samuel appointed Saul as Israel's first king. Saul was described as an impressive young man without equal, a foot taller than any other Israelite. He was thirty years old when he became king, and perhaps this led some of the people to have doubts about him. But their doubts soon faded away. Soon after Saul became king, the nasty Ammonite leader Nahash laid siege to the town of Jabesh and was planning to gouge out the right eyes of all the townsfolk. Saul lead 330,000 men in a predawn attack and destroyed the Ammonites.

Saul went on to other military successes, but his pride quickly got in the way of his leadership, and he fell out of God's favour. Samuel declared to him that his days as king were numbered and that another would take his place.

David

God chose a shepherd boy named David to be the next king. David was the youngest of seven brothers, described as "glowing with health and had a fine appearance and handsome features" (1 Samuel 16:12). David initially served

Saul as a musician in the king's court. But he really came into the public eye after a brave encounter during a military standoff with the enormous Philistine warrior Goliath, in which David killed Goliath with his shepherd's sling and then decapitated him.

David successfully led Israel in a series of military campaigns and soon became the hero of the people. If David lived today, he would be on the cover of *Time* magazine, and thousands of Internet fan-sites would be devoted to him. The paparazzi would follow him wherever he went, and the goss would be rife over who was his girlfriend. King Saul became increasingly jealous of David's popularity. He felt so threatened by David that he tried to kill him with a spear. David suddenly found himself sent on dangerous missions, during which Saul secretly hoped he would be killed. Men arrived at David's house to assassinate him. Saul's paranoia just got worse and worse. Eighty-five priests were killed and a town was destroyed because they helped David to escape.

Saul was demented with jealousy, and the future looked bleak for David. But in a military battle, Saul received a deadly wound and killed himself rather than let himself be captured. And so David finally took the throne. He was thirty years old.

For forty years, David was a strong and effective king. He captured the city of Jerusalem and settled there, making it the nation's capital and the home for the Israelite's valuable ark. The nation prospered and expanded as David met with success after success in his military campaigns.

But (yes, there's always a "but") David had his shortcomings. He slept with another man's wife (Bathsheba), and she became pregnant. To cover his tracks, he had her husband murdered by placing him in a dangerous position during a battle.

Things really got worse for David from there. His family was plagued by the kind of problems you would expect to see in a soap opera. His sons were involved in rape, incest and murder. One of them even conspired against David, sleeping with his concubines and leading a rebellion against David that ended in a battle with 20,000 casualties. Furthermore, David's firm grip on his rule as king seemed to slip as he made a number of bad decisions. Yet despite these failings, he is still remembered as Israel's great king.

> The nation prospered and expanded as David met with success after success in his military campaigns.

Solomon

Following David's death, his son Solomon became king in 970 BC, and under his reign, Israel enjoyed its greatest glory. The people lived in peace and were prosperous and happy. Solomon was wealthy beyond comprehension, a kind of ancient Bill Gates, except that Solomon had seven hundred wives and Bill Gates doesn't. An intelligent man and a scholar, Solomon was (and still is) famous for his wisdom, insight and knowledge. He authored thousands of proverbs (wise sayings) and wrote over a thousand songs.

The key feature of Solomon's reign was that he built an enormous temple for the Lord. No expense was spared for this outstanding architectural achievement, constructed out of the finest materials by the finest craftsmen. You can read the elaborate details in 1 Kings 5–8 and 2 Chronicles 2–5. The temple became the visible representation of God's presence and blessing. It was the heart of the nation of Israel, a place where God would live among his people in a permanent structure that was the finest building in the world. It gave the nation a focal point and was a symbol of their relationship with God.

From humble beginnings as a family in slavery, Israel had become a mighty nation of superiority and wealth. Yet like so many before him, Solomon turned away from God, and this glory period came to an end.

In those days, it was common for a man to have more than one wife. Solomon had seven hundred of them, not because he was a ladies' man but as the result of making shrewd political alliances with surrounding nations. Unfortunately, this contributed to his downfall. Many of Solomon's wives had no regard for God and brought with them their own temples and pagan rituals and beliefs. When Solomon grew old, some of his wives convinced him to worship the idols of Israel's neighbours. For all his wisdom, Solomon's zeal for God diminished, and his loyalty became divided between his wives and God. When Solomon died, the king with a divided heart left behind a divided kingdom.

> The temple became the visible representation of God's presence and blessing. It was the heart of the nation of Israel, a place where God would live among his people in a permanent structure that was the finest building in the world.

Where are we?

The 175-year narrative of the three kings follows the 335 years of rule by the judges. It is told in the History Books of 1 and 2 Samuel, 1 Kings and 1 and 2 Chronicles.

What time is it?

Samuel was born in 1105 BC. The lives and reigns of Saul, David and Solomon are traced through to the end of Solomon's reign in 930 BC.

In a nutshell

The period of King Saul, King David and King Solomon was one of the most prosperous and glorious for Israel. But while the kings were all intent on serving God, they also had their follies, including adultery, murder, idolatry and disobedience.

Who are the main people?

Eli (a high priest), Hannah (Samuel's mother), Samuel, Saul, David, Goliath, Jonathan (Saul's son and David's best friend), Bathsheba, Uriah (Bathsheba's husband), Solomon.

Miscellaneous

- David was a prolific songwriter. He wrote Psalm 40, which the Irish supergroup U2 turned into a number one song ("40").

- Next to Jesus, David is the most mentioned person in the Bible, coming in with 1,118 mentions.

- Solomon's temple was built by 30,000 labourers, 70,000 carriers and 80,000 stonecutters, as well as 3,300 supervisors.

Sometimes various groups within a country don't see eye to eye. This can lead to conflict, and in extreme cases, a nation can split into two.

Take the United States. They may be united now, but that wasn't always the case. Throughout the 1850s, hostility raged between the northern and southern states of America, largely revolving around the issue of slavery. It got so bad that in December 1860, South Carolina withdrew from the Union and was soon joined by ten other breakaway southern states. Calling themselves the Confederate States of America, they elected their own leader and capital city. America was divided into two factions, and for the next four years, a civil war raged within the country.

More recent examples of countries split by political or social conflicts are North and South Korea and the now reunified East and West Germany.

Israel suffered a similar division thousands of years ago. Under her first three kings – Saul, David and Solomon – Israel enjoyed a prosperous period of greatness. But that crumbled in Solomon's final years as he began to follow the false gods of some of his many wives.

After Solomon's death, the twelve tribes that made up Israel began to debate who would be the next king. Solomon's son Rehoboam came to the throne but soon proved to be a stern dictator, promising to rule harshly. The ten tribes of the north broke away from King Rehoboam and elected their own king, a bloke by the name of Jeroboam.* Jeroboam had been one of Solomon's officials, a powerful man who had run Solomon's labour force. And with Jeroboam's crowning, the nation of Israel, the descendants of Jacob's twelve sons, split into two factions.

Now, this gets a little confusing, so stay with us. The ten northern tribes kept the name Israel, even though technically all twelve tribes were still the nation of Israel. The two southern tribes were called Judah because Judah was the dominant tribe of the south. In short, the nation of Israel divided into two unequal parts:

- Ten tribes in the north led by Jeroboam (Solomon's official), which kept the name Israel. Their capital city was Samaria.

*Yes, it would be less confusing if Rehoboam and Jeroboam didn't sound so alike. It would be so much easier, for example, if they were called Robert and Jeremy.

- Two tribes in the south led by Rehoboam (Solomon's son), which called themselves Judah. Their capital city was Jerusalem.

A civil war seemed unavoidable. Judah (made up of the houses of Judah and Benjamin) immediately amassed a force of 180,000 fighting men to regain the throne. But through the prophet Shemaiah, God told them not to fight against their brothers. War was prevented.

The rest of 1 and 2 Kings covers the extensive twin histories of these two kingdoms and their fall from greatness. Both the northern and southern tribes began to slide into moral decay. Fighting and bickering between the two kingdoms became the norm, and the future began to look pretty grim for both of them.

In the north (Israel), things turned sour. Eighteen kings succeeded Jeroboam, and every one of them was corrupt. In most instances, the king came to power by murdering the one before him. Most notable of these was the evil King Ahab, who disregarded God's commandments and led Israel in worshiping Baal, a particularly nasty fertility figure of one of Israel's neighbours.

The picture was somewhat brighter in the south (Judah), where godly kings occasionally emerged. Of its twenty kings, eight of them sought to honour God. In the end, however, Judah followed the same path as the northern tribes, and Judah slid from God's favour as well. God's great nation had turned their back on him.

Amazingly, despite their rebellion, God remained faithful to his people. This was to be the era of the prophets. These were men and women who spoke on God's behalf and warned the people and their king of God's inevitable judgment if they continued to disobey him. Think of them as God's special task force of covenant police, a rescue team of spiritual commandos.

The first of these prophets was Elijah, who we first read about in 1 Kings 17. Elijah warned King Ahab of the devastating consequences of leading God's people into idolatry. But the king's encounters with Elijah proved to be fruitless, and Israel plummeted into further sin. Elijah was succeeded by Elisha, but his message also fell on deaf ears. (You can almost imagine God banging his head against the proverbial brick wall.) After Elijah and Elisha, God continued to raise up more prophets. Their writings and stories make up the last third of the Old Testament.

What was going to happen to these two kingdoms? Would they turn back to God and resolve their dispute over a king? Or would both nations continue to ignore God and end up in chaos? What would happen to those promises made to the forefathers of Israel all those years ago? Stay tuned and more will be revealed in the next chapter.

Amazingly, despite their rebellion, God remained faithful to his people.

Where are we?

We are about a third of the way through the Old Testament and well and truly on our way to finishing the History Books of the Old Testament.

What time is it?

First Kings begins with David's death and the start of Solomon's reign in 970 BC. Solomon died forty years later in 930 BC, and by the following year, the nation of Israel was divided. The books of 1 and 2 Kings and 2 Chronicles trace the history of these two kingdoms: the northern kingdom of Israel from 930 BC to 722 BC and the southern kingdom of Judah from 930 BC to 586 BC.

In a nutshell

The final chapters of 1 Kings and the first sixteen chapters of 2 Kings narrate Israel's division and subsequent downfall. As a result of King Solomon's idolatry and death, the twelve tribes of Israel split into two unequal groups. Ten tribes in the north kept the name Israel, while two tribes in the south became Judah. This marked the beginning of the end for both nations as evil and corrupt kings ruled and they fell further into idolatry.

Second Chronicles parallels 1 and 2 Kings but virtually ignores the northern kingdom of Israel because of its false worship and refusal to acknowledge the temple in Jerusalem.

Who are the main people?

Solomon, Jeroboam (ruler of Israel), Rehoboam (Solomon's son and ruler of Judah), the prophets Elijah and Elisha.

Miscellaneous

- The two books of Kings were originally one book, which was divided in two to make it more manageable on scrolls.

- Baal was the pagan god of fertility. Baal worship involved child sacrifice, prostitution, a lot of sexual carrying on and general lewdness around idols and phallic symbols.

- Pete's two favourite parts of the Bible are in the books of Kings. First, when Elijah had a contest with the 450 prophets of Baal (1 Kings 18). Massively outnumbered, he beat them and then had them all slaughtered. Second, when Elisha was taunted by a gang of youths who insulted him with the ancient equivalent of the words, "Get lost, baldy!" (2 Kings 2:23–25), Elisha cursed them, and then two bears came out of the woods and mauled the youths. The lessons here? Don't mess with the prophets of the Lord!

I magine for a moment a foreign nation invading your country.
Their armies roll in with tanks and planes, taking control of state after state until eventually they have occupied the northern half of your country. Soon all of the people living in those areas are herded up and exiled to a distant land, never to return. Then imagine about 130 years later they amass their forces and roll on into the remaining southern strongholds. Armies conquer the cities, and everyone is rounded up and taken away. Finally, the invading armies take over the remaining land, dismantle all the great buildings and cultural icons and confiscate them for their own purposes.

How would you feel watching your society, home and culture being dismantled? Imagine your feelings of loss, devastation and despair. This, in fact, is similar to what happened to the Israelites. Both the northern and southern kingdoms had been struggling. Eventually foreign armies invaded them, overtook the land, deported many of the Israelites and took most of their possessions for themselves. Israelite society crumbled.

The real beginning of this downfall had occurred much earlier. After Solomon died and the twelve tribes split into Israel and Judah, the people of God spiralled into full-scale rebellion. The crunch came (in 2 Kings 17–25) when the foreign empires of Assyria and later Babylon invaded, conquered and captured the cities and peoples of both the northern and southern kingdoms.

Of the two kingdoms, the northern kingdom of Israel was the worst. Not one of its nineteen kings honoured God. God had repeatedly warned Israel that continued sinfulness would lead to her destruction (1 Kings 9:4–9), and eventually his patience came to an end. While Israel grew weak because of its corrupt kings, Assyria, to the north of Israel, grew stronger. God allowed the Assyrians to conquer Israel (725 BC) and take away its inhabitants as part of his judgment on those who repeatedly disobeyed him. This spelt doom for their national character. The people would over time intermarry in a foreign land and, after a few generations, become absorbed by another nation. Those who were left behind intermarried with foreigners, and their children were, therefore, half-breed Israelites, known as Samaritans.

> God had repeatedly warned Israel that continued sinfulness would lead to her destruction, and eventually his patience came to an end.

The southern kingdom of Judah lasted longer than their northern neighbour but ultimately failed to learn from Israel's mistakes. In the end, they too faced God's wrath and were invaded by the Assyrians and finally by the Babylonians. The heart of Israelite society – the city of Jerusalem and the great temple – were plundered and destroyed in about 586 BC. Many of those who remained in Judah were taken into captivity. This program of deportation was a serious threat to the future of the Israelites. Those who left would, like their northern cousins, become absorbed into a foreign nation. Judah was resettled by foreigners who intermarried with the Israelites.

Little is known of what happened to these Israelites and what they did once they got to their new destinations. The Bible gives us a small amount of information about some of these prisoners and the emotions they experienced. Psalm 137 is a good example, in which the writer bitterly recalls weeping by the rivers of Babylon as they remembered their homeland. There their tormentors demanded the Israelites play them songs of joy, which was a bitter pill to swallow.

The main thing is that God's people had lost the precious signs that signified his favour – the land, the temple and their king. They took God for granted and rebelled against him despite repeated warnings. Then they paid the consequences. This period was the lowest era in Israel's history. The loss of their land, temple and independence shook the Israelites to the very core and should be a reminder to us all: *If you continue to reject God, eventually he will reject you, and you will forfeit his blessing.*

With Israel taken over and the people exiled to foreign lands, God's favour and his promises to Abraham must have seemed to disappear like a puff of smoke. To the Israelites living then, it must have seemed like the end of the world.

In the midst of this turmoil, however, was a small spark of hope. The exile did not mean a total end to God's people. Amazingly, God still intended to honour his promises. He continued to raise up prophets during these times, who explained why God's judgment had come. They also brought a glimmer of hope. Although it must have seemed impossible, in time God would restore the Israelites, both physically and spiritually.

But how that would happen was yet to be seen.

If you continue to reject God, eventually he will reject you, and you will forfeit his blessing.

Where are we?

Assyria's invasion of Israel is recorded in 2 Kings 17–18. The remaining chapters of 2 Kings narrate the successive kings of Judah and its ultimate downfall to the Babylonians. We also learn something about this period from the prophetic books of Ezekiel, Jeremiah and Daniel. We are approaching the end of the History Books of the Old Testament.

What time is it?

The northern kingdom of Israel was invaded by Assyria in 725 BC and ultimately fell in 722 BC, after which most of its inhabitants were deported. The southern kingdom of Judah lasted approximately another 136 years before eventually falling to the Babylonians by 586 BC.

In a nutshell

Despite God's repeated warnings through a number of prophets that if the Israelites failed to keep his commandments, they would face his judgment, they continued to sin and ended up facing some pretty heavy consequences. The northern kingdom and eventually the southern kingdom were invaded by the Assyrians and the Babylonians. Both kingdoms lost God's blessing and, as a result, lost the benefits of his favour. It was the lowest point of Israel's history.

Who are the main people?

Among others, the kings Hezekiah, Manasseh, Josiah, Hoshea, Nebuchadnezzar, Jeroboam II, Shalmaneser V, Jehoiachin. The prophets Ezekiel, Jeremiah, Daniel.

Miscellaneous

- Israel had nineteen kings after Solomon, while Judah had twenty.

- Manasseh was twelve years old and Josiah eight years old when they became kings of Judah.

- The temple was destroyed by fire when the Babylonians invaded Jerusalem in 586 BC.

- The Jews despised and were openly hostile to the Samaritans because they were half-breeds. In John 4:1–26, a Samaritan woman is shocked when the unthinkable happens and Jesus (a Jew) asks her (a Samaritan) for a drink. Normally, Jews would not use even a dish a Samaritan had used. In fact, they wouldn't even speak the word Samaritan!

- Psalm 137 was made into a chart-topping pop song by Boney-M in the 1970s.

The Manly Sea Eagles were one of the great Australian rugby league clubs of the 1970s and 1980s.

But in the year 2000, this once great club was overthrown and absorbed and taken north of Sydney as part of a merged new team under the new name Northern Eagles. Their leaders were removed from power. Fans were devastated as the once great Brookvale Oval fell silent and years of history drifted north in the wind. The name of the Manly Sea Eagles had gone forever. Or had it?

In 2002, after a few years in the rugby league wilderness, the venture failed and the Eagles returned to their old home. At the first game, a group of fans stormed the northern hill and symbolically claimed it with their old flag. The local council injected hundreds of thousands of dollars to improve the ground. T-shirts and websites sprang up, proudly declaring "We're Back!" There was great celebration and excitement all around as the players and fans re-established themselves under their old name in their original home.

We are scraping the bottom of the barrel here drawing links between rugby league clubs and the history of Israel, but hopefully you get the picture. The kingdoms of Israel and Judah couldn't get much lower. They had been overthrown by Assyria and then by the Babylonians. Much of the city of Jerusalem had been destroyed. Their leaders had been removed from power, and the Israelites had lost their land, their temple and, most significantly, the blessings of God.

God never abandoned his people, however. The books of Ezra, Nehemiah and Esther record one of God's greatest acts of kindness. God began to work on the hearts of men and women to bring about a brand-new day in Israel's history. Amazingly, after seventy years of captivity in Babylon, the Israelites were allowed to return home to rebuild their lives.

Lots had happened since the Israelites had been taken from their homeland. The book of Ezra begins seventy years after the end of the previous book of 2 Chronicles, with Persia having conquered the Babylonians and Cyrus crowned as Persia's new king. In accordance with the prophecy made by Jeremiah years before, God stirred Cyrus's heart so dramatically that in his first

> God began to work on the hearts of men and women to bring about a brand-new day in Israel's history.

year as king, he allowed the Israelites to return to their Promised Land and rebuild their lives.

You can barely imagine the excitement and sense of expectation after all that time as the first Israelites made their journey home, apparently all wearing their "We're Back!" T-shirts. But it wasn't going to be easy. Their great city was no longer what it once was. The city of Jerusalem and the temple had fallen into a state of disrepair due to the ravages of invasion, occupation and years of neglect. There was a lot of work to be done.

The exiles began to return from Babylon, but not all at once. Over a period of about one hundred years, a small number of the remaining faithful Israelites returned in three separate journeys. The book of Ezra narrates the first two of these returns from Babylon. The first return was led by Zerubbabel, who subsequently rebuilt the temple and restored the religious feasts. Ezra the priest, who was a real mover and shaker, led the second. Ezra encouraged and led the people in re-establishing their devotion to God and his commandments. If Ezra were around today, he would be a motivational speaker on the international circuit.

Not all went smoothly. Considerable opposition from the new occupants of the land gave the returning Israelites a lot of headaches. Furthermore, the Israelites themselves continued to disobey God, and the whole restoration process stalled a number of times. Strikes and threats from their neighbours jeopardised construction work. There were stop-work actions and picket lines all over the place. Subversive activists tried to undermine the project by suggesting the temple would disrupt the community. The tough conditions and opposition meant that the people's enthusiasm died, and construction stopped for a time. Nevertheless, despite the opposition, the building of the walls and temple eventually got back on track, largely due to men like Ezra.

The story of Esther took place in the fifty-eight-year gap between the two journeys (recorded in Ezra 6 and 7). It narrates the story of Esther, one of many Jews who remained behind. She became queen of Persia and was instrumental in the survival of Jews who remained behind. Esther is a great story of treachery and intrigue and of God's will prevailing.

The third and final return of the Jews is recorded in the book of Nehemiah. Nehemiah led a group of Israelites back to Jerusalem thirteen years after Ezra's journey. Upon his return, Nehemiah oversaw the rebuilding of Jerusalem's city walls. This did not run smoothly either. The returnees continued to sin, and they came up against repeated opposition. But eventually, after the preaching and pleading of Ezra and Nehemiah, the city and temple were rebuilt and their religious customs reinstated.

All of this leaves you wondering. Had Israel truly been reborn, or were they going to fail God again? Even though the temple had been rebuilt, it was not the same as in its glory days under Solomon. Was there ever going to be a day when Israel would truly be a great nation and a light to the rest of the world?

Had Israel truly been reborn, or were they going to fail God again?

Where are we?

The return of the Israelites marks the end of the History Books. Ezra, Nehemiah and Esther come after 1 and 2 Chronicles and before the Wisdom and Poetry Books, which begin with the story of Job.

What time is it?

The books of Ezra, Nehemiah and Esther cover a period of about one hundred years. The Persians invaded Babylon in 539 BC, and in the following year, Cyrus's decree permitted the exiles to return and rebuild Jerusalem. The temple was rebuilt in 520 BC, and the walls of Jerusalem were completed by 445 BC. A number of faithful Israelites returned to the Promised Land during this period in three separate journeys. The first in 538–516 BC, the second in 458–457 BC and the last in 444–425 BC.

In a nutshell

God used certain men and women to bring about a decree that allowed the Israelites to return to their land after seventy years of captivity. The books of Ezra, Nehemiah and Esther record the triumphs and failures of the returning Israelites and the rebuilding of the city and temple of Jerusalem.

Who are the main people?

Ezra (priest and scribe), Cyrus (king of Persia), the prophets Haggai and Zechariah, Nehemiah (originally cupbearer to the king of Persia, later governor of Judah), Darius I (king of Persia), Artaxerxes (king of Persia), Esther (queen of Persia).

Miscellaneous

- Esther is one of only two books to be named after a female. The other is Ruth.

- Prior to becoming a world-class leader and builder, Nehemiah's job was to test the king's wine to make sure it was not poisoned. As the king's life was literally in the wine taster's hands, this was an important job that displayed a high level of trust.

- The wall took fifty-two days to rebuild.

- Esther is one of only two books of the Bible that does not mention the name of God.

- The books of Ezra and Nehemiah were originally treated as one book. They were first split into two in the early third century AD. The Wycliffe Bible (1382) referred to the book of Ezra as 1 Ezdras and the book of Nehemiah as 2 Ezdras.

Chapter 26

THE DEAD POETS
Songs and poems from God's people
Psalms, Song of Songs

Many years ago before we knew each other, we (as in Ben and Pete) were coincidentally at the same rock concert. It was U2's Unforgettable Fire world tour, and at the end of the show, the band pulled off their signature finish by performing their song "40". One by one, the instruments petered out and the lights dimmed, leaving the two of us, along with 11,998 other fans belting out the mournful lyrics in the darkness.*

Most of the concertgoers wouldn't have been aware that that very song was a bit of a slap-together job. When U2 was recording their 1983 album *War*, they needed one more song, but they were already a week overdue with studio time. The story goes that lead singer Bono pulled out his Bible and read these words:

> I waited patiently for the LORD;
>   he turned to me and heard my cry.
> He lifted me out of the slimy pit,
>   out of the mud and mire;
> he set my feet on a rock
>   and gave me a firm place to stand.
> He put a new song in my mouth,
>   a hymn of praise to our God.
> Many will see and fear the LORD
>   and put their trust in him.
>   – PSALM 40:1–3

They hammered out a tune, and the rest is history. It's amazing to think that U2's "40" is actually Psalm 40, and that 12,000 of us were singing lyrics written thousands of years ago by King David.

Psalms

The book of Psalms is an ancient anthology of 150 songs originally set to music. Think of it as a compilation box set of CDs of great prayer and praise songs.

Songs are a great medium of communication. You probably have a few favourites that you like to listen to and sing in the shower. Some songs touch

> *That was one of the best concerts I've ever been to.   – Ben
>
> Yeah, I've still got the T-shirt!   – Pete
>
> Me too. But mine still fits.   – Ben

your heart and make you feel sad. Others are stirring and make you hammer an air guitar behind a closed door. And some songs, like house music, make you want to stick your fingers in your ears and scream out "Make it stop, please mummy, make it stoooooopppp!!!!!!!" Psalms are songs too, and they help us to express our feelings toward God. They communicate just about every kind of emotion – fear and love, confusion and anger, hope and praise, desperation and gratitude.

Many of the psalms were written in times of sadness, and we hear the regret or grief that the author felt at the time. A classic is Psalm 51, in which King David speaks of his regret for having slept with Bathsheba (another man's wife) and his order to have her husband killed. You can imagine how low this great man of God felt about that incident. Hence, this psalm is sometimes termed the "Blues of the Bible".

Many of these poetic songs are uplifting and full of joy, however. They praise and thank God for who he is or for something he has done. "Glorify the LORD with me; let us exalt his name together. I sought the LORD, and he answered me; he delivered me from all my fears," says Psalm 34 (with screaming air guitar). It is in this sense that the psalms teach us how to pray and to praise God.

In many ways, the psalms are the most intimate words of the Bible, as they take us to every depth of human emotion. They give us a window into the thoughts and feelings of the faithful people of God who lived throughout the rise and fall of Israel. Their words are timeless, and throughout the years, they have been a source of great comfort and hope to the millions who read and sing them.

Song of Songs

Song of Songs (sometimes called "Song of Solomon") has been described as the "sealed section of the Bible". Jewish boys in ancient times were not allowed to read this book. Pretty raunchy, eh?

The book is basically a conversational love letter, filled with poetry that is passionate, intimate and, at times, very sensual. Some of it is admittedly a little hard for us to understand. Try drawing a picture of this ideal woman using the components described in Song of Songs, and you will see what we mean. With doves for eyes, hair like a flock of goats, the tower of Babylon for a nose, teeth like a flock of sheep, and two fawns for breasts, she is not the kind of woman you would want to bump into in a dark alley. The descriptions may seem a bit odd to us but were huge compliments in that ancient culture! Overall, it is a beautiful book showing us the intimacy, devotion and love that God desires a couple to have. It also shows us that God is not a prude! Sex and passion are gifts for a man and woman to enjoy in a committed relationship.

Psalms teach us how to pray and to praise God.

Where are we?

We have left the History Books of the Old Testament and are doubling back to some of the creative writings, wisdom sayings and prophets that emerged in the period from King David (around 1000 BC) through to the return from exile (around 500 BC). The Poetry Books of the Old Testament come after the History Books (Genesis to Esther) and before the Prophetic Books (Isaiah to Malachi). They cross over and often relate to the historical events described in the books of Samuel, Kings and Chronicles.

What time is it?

King David, who reigned around 1000 BC, wrote most of the psalms. Some psalms, however, may have been written as much as five hundred years later. Traditionally, King Solomon is credited as being the author of Song of Songs although we really don't know. If Solomon was the author, he most likely would have written Song of Songs around the years 965–955 BC.

In a nutshell

Psalms is the songbook of the Bible, containing 150 songs expressing a wide variety of human emotions. Song of Songs is a passionate and intimate love poem between two lovers and is a great example of the loving relationships that God wants us to have.

Who are the main people?

King David and his son King Solomon.

Miscellaneous

- Solomon is said to have written over a thousand songs (1 Kings 4:32), which is more than Elvis Presley wrote!

- The word *psalm* comes from the Greek word *psalmos*, meaning "song" or "hymn". The letters *P* and *L* in *Psalms* are silent, so it sounds like SARMS, not puh-SALL-ems.

- Psalms is the longest and possibly the most widely read book in the Bible. It is the second-most-quoted Old Testament book in the New Testament (414 times).

- The British playwright and poet William Shakespeare turned forty-seven in 1611, the year the King James Version was released. In this version, the forty-sixth word of Psalm 46 is *shake*, and the forty-seventh word from the end of Psalm 46 is *spear*. (Some people have too much time on their hands.) Coincidentally, in the New International Version, the forty-sixth word of Psalm 46 is *Selah*, and the forty-seventh word from the end of Psalm 46 is *bow*, and there is, amazingly, no famous playwright named Selahbow.

- One of Pete's friends had his wife's wedding ring engraved with the verse reference "Songs 8:7". His wife got very upset when she looked up the verse. The guy couldn't understand why, until he looked at the ring. It had been engraved incorrectly as "Songs 7:8" instead of 8:7. Look it up and you'll understand.

- Song of Songs is one of only two books in the Bible that doesn't contain the name of God.

Chapter 27

SPEAKING WORDS OF WISDOM
The Wisdom Books
Job, Proverbs, Ecclesiastes

What are the most popular books around today?

You would be correct if you said romance fiction. And crime fiction is certainly up there too. But all you have to do is go to amazon.com or your local bookshop to see how self-improvement books have become the literary hot stuff of the twenty-first century.

Gurus of modern living and self-improvement write this "modern wisdom" literature. What these books offer, in one way or another, is practical know-how about life. Wisdom is basically skill in living, knowing how to order one's life, be successful and have sound relationships. Every week books are published that will teach you how to be happy, lose weight, be financially secure, have better relationships, find yourself, heal yourself, improve yourself, cook like a chef, structure your work environment, make a million dollars in just one year, be a better parent, be a better spouse, be at peace, be bop-a-lula, win friends and influence people and pretty well any other conceivable topic that you can begin a title with *How to . . .* or *Ten Steps to . . .* or *The Dummies' Guide to . . .*

This kind of literature is nothing new. Israel had its fair share of wise sayings and stories aimed at teaching readers about living an effective and prosperous life. These writings came from a variety of wise men and women and are scattered throughout the Bible. Three books in the Old Testament, however, are so rich in this type of literature that they are referred to as Wisdom Books. They are the books of Job, Proverbs and Ecclesiastes.

Wisdom is all about making good decisions and living a life that is pleasing to God. One of the most important recurring phrases in the Wisdom Books is "the fear of the Lord". This term means "reverent awe and respect for God". Each book contains the phrase, and all of them emphasize a healthy fear and respect for God as being essential for having a well-rounded and balanced life.

Job

The story of Job is one of the most fascinating, and perhaps even controversial, books of the Bible. It tells of Job, a wealthy, successful and godly bloke with a

> Wisdom is all about making good decisions and living a life that is pleasing to God.

wife and ten children. But in a single day, all of his livestock were lost and all of his children were killed by a freak wind. Shortly after that, he was inflicted with painful boils over his entire body. Things were rock bottom for Job.

This book confronts us with the reality that sometimes good people suffer, and sometimes evil and calamity seem to succeed. As we read of Job, we can also think of people we know who are suffering or situations in life in which things have gone terribly, terribly wrong, and life, quite simply, does not seem fair.

How would you feel if you were Job? Angry? Bitter? Vengeful? Job's wife sure did. She wanted Job to curse God for their suffering, but Job remained faithful, saying that he would follow God in the bad times, not just the good. The book is largely a series of conversations Job had with a number of his friends as they pondered and tried to explain his terrible suffering. At the end of the book, God spoke to Job in a long series of questions. These questions made Job realise that he should let God be God. (You'll be pleased to know there is a semi-happy ending, as Job is blessed with wealth, children and old age.)

Proverbs

The book of Proverbs is a collection of hundreds of practical statements written "for gaining wisdom and instruction; for understanding words of insight; for receiving instruction in prudent behaviour, doing what is right and just and fair" (Proverbs 1:2–3). The book paints a picture showing that wisdom leads to success and happiness, while a lack of wisdom leads to sorrow and trouble.

We are used to the type of statements we see on desk calendars: "Look before you leap" or "A bird in the hand is worth two in the bush" or "Give a man a fish, and he'll eat for a day. Teach him how to fish and he'll eat forever". Then there are the less well-known ones: "Do not use a hatchet to remove a fly from your friend's forehead" or "Don't answer the phone when you have a hot iron in your hand".

> The book of Proverbs contains a variety of types of wise sayings on almost every universal topic. Its sayings are as valid and applicable to us today as they were way back then.

The book of Proverbs contains a variety of types of wise sayings on almost every universal topic. Its sayings are as valid and applicable to us today as they were way back then. While not quite the Ten Commandments, these proverbs help us reflect on human life. They teach us about fear, love, prosperity, poverty, marriage, business, finance, adultery, laziness, foolish behaviour, ethics, work, family, violence, discipline, slander, self-control, forgiveness and general living. Some proverbs seem mundane: "If you find honey, eat just enough – too much of it, and you will vomit" (25:16); while others are blunt: "Keep to a path far from [the adulteress], do not go near the door of her house" (5:8).

What makes this collection of proverbs different from any other of its kind in the ancient world is that they were specifically inspired by God through the lives of a number of men, most notably King Solomon. Solomon was considered one of the wisest men of the ancient world. His wisdom thus inspired as many as three thousand proverbs and over a thousand songs.

Ecclesiastes

Have you ever been in a reflective mood and wondered what life is all about and asked yourself why you spend so much time working and striving and struggling when at the end of the road you die? Sometimes it seems like it's all pointless and for nothing – all the building and gathering of possessions and studying and going to work and putting extensions on our houses and pursuing love and trying to make a difference.

The writer of Ecclesiastes had those feelings too. (Although it's not certain, many believe that the author was King Solomon.) This short book is written from the perspective of an extremely wealthy man who looks back on the meaning and purpose of life. He had searched for meaning in various avenues – knowledge, hard work, wealth and the pursuit of pleasure – but had found only "meaninglessness" in all his endeavours. He had built gardens and parks and houses, owned slaves and a harem and accumulated tremendous amounts of silver and gold. But on looking back, he realised that it was all meaningless, a "chasing after the wind". He finds life confusing and perplexing, mysterious and contradictory.

This doesn't mean, however, that we should all just lie down and stare at the wall all day. His final conclusion is positive: enjoy the life that God has given you and "fear God and keep his commandments". The world can be enjoyed, but true meaning comes from a relationship with God.

> The world can be enjoyed, but true meaning comes from a relationship with God.

Where are we?

The Wisdom Books lie roughly in the middle of the Bible, between the History Books and the Prophetic Books of the Old Testament.

What time is it?

It is believed by some that King Solomon penned most of the proverbs and the book of Ecclesiastes during his reign as king of Israel. If that was the case, these two books would have been written sometime between 970 and 930 BC. It is not known when the book of Job was written, but it is believed to have been written before any other book of the Bible.

In a nutshell

The Wisdom Books contain the wise sayings of the wise men of Israel, most notably King Solomon. The major theme of all these books is to "fear God" in all circumstances.

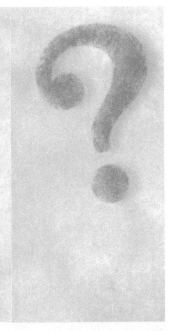

Who are the main people?

Solomon, Job and his friends Eliphaz, Bildad, Zophar and Elihu.

Miscellaneous

- Many scholars believe that Job is the oldest book of the Bible. It is possible that Job was a contemporary of Abraham.

- One of Ben's favourite wise sayings comes from the pen of Solomon in the book of Proverbs: "Like a gold ring in a pig's snout is a beautiful woman who shows no discretion" (11:22).

- Job is pronounced "Jobe" (as in "robe").

- The folk song "Turn, Turn, Turn", made popular by the Byrds in 1973, is taken from Ecclesiastes 3.

- One of the most popular "wisdom" books today is Stephen Covey's *The Seven Habits of Highly Effective People*, with sales over 10 million. Interestingly, at the end of his book, Covey states, "I believe that correct principles are natural laws, and that God, the Creator and Father of us all, is the source of them".[1]

---

1. Stephen R. Covey, *The Seven Habits of Highly Effective People* (New York: Simon and Schuster, 1989), 319.

Chapter 28

MEN OF GREAT VOICE
The prophets speak

Isaiah, Jeremiah, Lamentations, Ezekiel, Daniel, Hosea, Joel, Amos, Obadiah, Jonah, Micah, Nahum, Habakkuk, Zephaniah, Haggai, Zechariah, Malachi

Back in the History Books of the Old Testament, we read that the nation of Israel was unable to be faithful to God.

Between 1000 BC and 400 BC, Israel increasingly moved away from God and began to follow the ways of their ungodly neighbours. Understandably, God wasn't too happy about this. So he sent men on a special mission to tell the rulers and the people what God was thinking and what he was doing or about to do. These men, these spiritual commandos, were the X-men . . . we mean, these men were the prophets.

A crusty old man with a beard and a robe stands on a wooden crate at the city gates. "Repent ye sinners, for the kingdom of God is at hand!" he cries, laughing maniacally, shaking a knobbly finger at all who pass by.

Sound familiar? This is the picture many people have in mind when they hear the word *prophet.* Yet the prophets were diverse. Amos was a shepherd and a keeper of sycamore trees. Jeremiah was a priest. Isaiah was a court advisor. Zephaniah was a man of standing, perhaps even of royal blood. Jonah didn't want to be a prophet at all! What they had in common, however, was that they all spoke to the people about obedience, judgment and hope.

Many people give up reading when they reach the last seventeen books of the Old Testament (the Prophetic Books). Some of the prophets' words can seem a little confusing and repetitive, outdated and irrelevant to life today. Little wonder that the least read books of the Bible are Isaiah through Malachi. But don't skip these amazing books. In many ways, the prophets are the most "modern" writers of the Bible. They deal with the same issues that confront us today: the silence of God when there is pain, economic disparity, injustice, war, relentless suffering, loss of meaning and disillusionment. But most important, these books give us tremendous insight into the heart of God: what makes him happy and what makes him angry; what he does with those who rebel against him and how he reacts to those who love him; how to have a relationship with him and how to come back to him if that relationship is broken.

One of the prophets' main themes is *judgment.* Many of their words take the form of warnings, spoken during the days when Israel was divided into two nations or when the Israelites were being conquered by other nations. The

> The Prophetic Books deal with the same issues that confront us today. But most important, these books give us tremendous insight into the heart of God.

prophets were trying to get across the message that God was not happy when the Israelites ignored him and that punishment was inevitable, unless they pulled their heads in and got their act together. Pretty serious stuff, eh?

The prophets were not all doom and gloom, however. Another important element of their message was *hope.* Almost all of the prophets brought some good news. They spoke of a future time when all would be made well, a time when God would restore all things and when the promises made to Abraham would be fulfilled completely.

And so for many Jews at the time of Jesus (four hundred years later), the prophets were the most studied and debated books of the day. *If God is going to restore our nation, how will it happen? Who will bring about restoration? And what will happen when it comes?*

At a low point in Israel's history, the prophets pointed to a new hope in God, and their books conclude the Old Testament with great expectations that God was about to do something really big, but the question is *what?*

Isaiah

The prophets were men with an important job who spoke on God's behalf in troubled times. As the books written by these men make up such a large and significant part of the Bible, it is important that we don't skip over them too quickly. So before we move on, let's have a closer look at one of the Prophetic Books.

If the prophets had their own bubble-gum cards, Isaiah would be the one everyone would want to own. Many people say he was *the* great prophet. His book is one of the longest in the Bible, and it contains some of the most remarkable prophecies about Jesus and the future kingdom that appear in the Old Testament.

Isaiah was a married bloke with a family. (One of his sons – Maher-Sha-lal-Hash-Baz – has the unique privilege of having the longest name in the Bible.) Isaiah preached around two hundred years after the glory days of King David and King Solomon (approximately 740–680 BC). By the time Isaiah arrived on the scene, Israel was already in its darkest days. The once great kingdom had split into two. Israel and Judah had abandoned God, and their leaders were becoming increasingly corrupt. The Assyrians had already invaded Israel, and it was only a matter of time before Judah would face the same fate. Isaiah spoke mainly to the southern tribes (Judah) in the final days before they too were invaded.

Like most of the prophets, Isaiah essentially had two things to say to the Israelites:

1. He warned them that because of their disobedience, God's judgment was inevitable. Like the northern tribes, the southern tribes would be

> The prophets were men with an important job who spoke on God's behalf in troubled times.

invaded and would lose their land, their temple, their identity, their freedom and God's blessings. Isaiah did not beat about the bush. He used frightening and disturbing language. He spoke bluntly of God's anger and wrath and of days of darkness, terror, pain and anguish.

2. Isaiah also offered great hope, however. He spoke of God's compassion and willingness to forgive. He told the Israelites that a time would come when God would restore those who were faithful to him and give them a place to live, with all the blessings that come with his favour. Isaiah spoke of great banquets, joyful singing, victories and endless happiness.

Some of Isaiah's most exciting words were his prophecies about the arrival of a Saviour. Many modern films have adopted this idea. In the Bruce Willis extravaganza *The Fifth Element*, the priests foretell of the coming of one (Leeloo) who will save the universe. Similarly, the popular *Matrix* series has its oracle telling of the coming of a saviour in the form of Neo. Thousands of years before, however, Isaiah was preaching about the coming of the real Saviour.

Isaiah foretold of one who would bring about restoration among God's people. He said that a child would be born under miraculous circumstances: "Therefore the Lord himself will give you a sign: The virgin will conceive and give birth to a son, and will call him Immanuel" (Isaiah 7:14). Even the title of the Saviour – **Immanuel,** which means "God with us" – hints at God's grace and willingness to save his people.

This promised Saviour would be called "Wonderful Counselor, Mighty God, Everlasting Father, Prince of Peace" (Isaiah 9:6). Isaiah went on to say that this Saviour would "reign on David's throne and over his kingdom, establishing and upholding it with justice and righteousness from that time on and forever" (Isaiah 9:7).

In addition, with remarkable precision, Isaiah predicted the death of this Chosen One in what have become some of the most famous words of the Bible:

> He was pierced for our transgressions, he was crushed for our iniquities; the punishment that brought us peace was on him, and by his wounds we are healed. We all, like sheep, have gone astray, each of us has turned to our own way; and the LORD has laid on him the iniquity of us all.
>
> – *Isaiah 53:5–6*

And then one day, a star shone bright in the night sky, and in a quiet little town, a baby was born.

For several hundred years, generation after generation of Israelites watched and waited for the coming of this Promised One, the Saviour. And then one day, a star shone bright in the night sky, and in a quiet little town, a baby was born.

Here we will turn our attention to the New Testament and read about the arrival of the Promised One. It is there that we read of Immanuel, "God with us", the Saviour of the world – Jesus.

Where are we?

The seventeen books of the prophets come after the Wisdom and Poetry Books and stretch from Isaiah through to Malachi, concluding the Old Testament. They represent almost half of the books and a third of the content of the Old Testament.

What time is it?

The prophets arrived on the scene when the Israelites were becoming morally bankrupt and moving away from God and his ways. The era of the prophets began around 1000 BC, during the reign of King David, and went through to about 400 BC, when some of the Israelites returned to rebuild the city and temple (as recorded in Ezra and Nehemiah).

In a nutshell

The prophets were men whom God inspired to speak to the people about their relationship with him and what he was about to do. They spoke of judgment and hope.

Who are the main people?

The main prophets were Isaiah, Jeremiah, Ezekiel and Daniel. Other prophets worth mentioning who spoke during this period are Elijah and Elisha, although these two don't have their own books. You can read about them in 1 and 2 Kings.

Miscellaneous

- The book of Isaiah is the longest Prophetic Book. It is the Old Testament book most quoted in the New Testament (419 times) and is quoted in twenty-three books.

- Ben wanted to name his cat Habakkuk, but his wife wouldn't let him.

- Maher-Shalal-Hash-Baz is the longest name in the Bible. It is mentioned in Isaiah 8:1.

- Obadiah is the shortest book in the Old Testament.

- The prophet Hosea was married to an "adulterous woman". His love for his unfaithful wife was seen as a symbol of God's love for his unfaithful people.

- Isaiah's name means "the Lord saves". Some sources claim that he was killed by being placed in a log that was then sawn in half.

The final book of the Old Testament is Malachi. When you read the last words of the book and turn the page, you find yourself in the next book, called Matthew.

Somewhere in your subconscious, you probably think that Matthew takes up where Malachi left off or at the very least that Matthew was written one or two years after Malachi. But this is not the case. In that one second it takes to turn the page, the Bible jumps four hundred years into the future. On the last page of Malachi, you're in about 400 BC, and then you turn the page, and suddenly it is the time of Jesus – four hundred years later! *How come?*

The authors of the books of the Bible weren't just recording random events of history. Rather, they recorded *what God was doing* in history – his thoughts, words and actions – and people's subsequent responses. It seems that God was silent for about four hundred years. That's not to say he was off sleeping somewhere or that he'd run out of ideas, but he had finished speaking through his prophets and waited for the right time to finally speak and act.

Much happened in the ancient world during this period, however, that is worth mentioning, as it helps us understand the context of the New Testament and the society and culture in which Jesus lived.

The Political Situation

When some of the Israelites returned to their land to rebuild Jerusalem and the temple, they did it with the permission of the king of the Persian Empire, which had overthrown the Babylonians. When they arrived, however, their land was not restored to the mighty empire they had expected. Rather than being a shining beacon to other countries, Israel was a backwater province of little importance to the Persians. The Israelites were not permitted to have a king, and they still had to pay taxes to the Persians. Many of the people had lost faith and hope. They thought God had abandoned them. Their worship had become dry and stale. The great promises made to their ancestors seemed to have disappeared like dust in the wind. And that is where the Old Testament finishes.

If the Old Testament was a movie, you'd stand up in the cinema and yell, "Hang on a sec . . . it can't finish like that! What sort of ending is *that*? Where's the wrap-up? Where's the conclusion?" Then you'd look up on the screen and see the words "To be continued", and you would realise that it was just part 1 of a two-part movie series.

When you like a movie series, like *Star Wars* or *The Lord of the Rings* or *The Matrix* or maybe even *Police Academy*, you have a great sense of anticipation between the films. It is agonizing waiting years for the next instalment to be made and released.

Four hundred years passed before the Old Testament's sequel – the New Testament – was written. And during that time, just when you thought it couldn't get any worse for God's people, they were out of the frying pan and into the fire.

As time marched on, sporadic revolts were staged in several regions throughout the empire. Persian rulers came and went, but none of them were able to fully stamp out the fighting. So, like the Babylonians, the Persians failed to sustain control over every region. About one hundred years later, their empire began to crumble.

The final nail in the coffin of the Persian Empire came with Alexander the Great. In 334 BC, together with 35,000 soldiers, Alexander began a series of battles that would methodically destroy the Persians and establish in his wake the greatest empire the civilized world had ever seen. Unique in military history, Alexander was undefeated in battle. Bit by bit, through almost 32,000 kilometres* of sieges and battles, his world expanded under the feet of the Greek army. Alexander took over Babylon and all the great Persian cities, as well as Egypt and India. He destroyed towns, took prisoners by the tens of thousands and built his own cities. Provinces and countries fell before him until this twenty-seven-year-old leader had conquered 90 percent of the known world. Beginning in 330 BC, his empire would reign supreme for almost three hundred years.

Alexander took control of the empire at the tender age of twenty. Like the Persians, Alexander allowed the Jews to remain in their homeland and gave them permission to practise their religious customs. When Alexander died, his instructions for a successor were unclear. As a result, not one but four co-leaders ruled the empire, which they divided into twenty regions. Throughout the years that followed, more fighting and revolts continued as different leaders came and went.

By the time we reach the first pages of the New Testament and the world of the first century AD, a new empire ruled and occupied the Promised Land and much of the known world. Throughout the century before the birth of Jesus, the Romans had become the dominant force in the ancient world, thanks largely to their ruler named Pompey. The Romans flexed their military might and soon ruled most of the Western world.

Throughout this four-hundred-year period, the Jews continued to rebuild their cities and homes. Many, however, were frustrated that things were not

Four hundred years passed before the Old Testament's sequel – the New Testament – was written.

*Almost 22,000 miles.

like they used to be when David and Solomon ruled. Foreign rulers who had little regard for God and his commands were governing Israel. As a result, pockets of resistance arose from militant Jews who sought independence from outside rulers. Bloody battles ensued, and in some cases, many lives were lost as Jews fought for self-rule. But none of these battles was successful.

The Jewish Religious Situation

As far as the religious situation among the Israelites is concerned, the most notable change was that there was no monarchy. The new ruler of Israel was not a king but the high priest. He became the so-called religious and civic head of the Jewish community, bowing only to the authority of the secular rulers. Unfortunately, this position was abused, so that by the first century, high priests were often corrupted by the power they wielded.

God's people struggled to maintain their religion, under heavy persecution from foreign powers. The Greeks tried to force their religion and ways upon the Israelites. Copies of their holy writings (the Old Testament) were destroyed, gold from their temple was sold and people were forced to worship Greek gods. Tens of thousands were killed when the evil Antiochus Epiphanes (one of the last kings of the Greek empire, who ruled from 175 to 164 BC) crushed a rebellion. He was an evil ruler, a kind of ancient Hitler, who ordered the slaughter of innocent women and children. Even the name he gave himself hints at his arrogance.* Antiochus set up a statue of the Greek god Zeus in the temple and further horrified the people when he sacrificed a pig there. He made the pig into a soup and sprinkled it all over the temple. Because the Jews considered the pig an unclean animal, this was perhaps the most offensive and degrading thing that could have been done to them. This pushed the Jewish people over the brink, and opposition to Antiochus flared up. An elderly villager named Mattathias, along with his five sons, led a revolt against him. A twenty-four-year war, known as the **Maccabean Revolt,** followed, resulting in the independence of Judah for approximately eighty years, until the Romans took control in 63 BC.

Unfortunately, the Romans also persecuted the Jews and made it difficult for them to practise their devotion to God. In 63 BC, Pompey entered Jerusalem after a three-month siege, murdered the priest in the temple and entered the Most Holy Place. The Jewish people would never forgive the Romans for this sacrilege. During this period, a number of Jews became disenchanted with Israel's leadership and its direction, both politically and spiritually. Several factions formed, each with their own views on the religious and political ideals for Israel, so that by the time we reach the world of the first century, a number of Jewish sects existed within the community. The *Pharisees* were almost pathologically dedicated to following God's law. In fact, they were so pious and strict about following the law that they added laws of their

> God's people struggled to maintain their religion, under heavy persecution from foreign powers.

*Epiphanes means "divine manifestation".

own just to be sure. The **Sadducees** were wealthy priests who controlled the Jewish ruling council and benefited from the Roman occupation.

Another important development during this period was the progression of the final form of the Old Testament. Many faithful Israelites saw the need to have a guide on how they were to live and honour God. They began to collect all the traditional writings they considered to be the inspired words of God. Once this was done, the entire body of traditional writings was edited into what eventually became the Hebrew canon of scriptures. This compilation and editing process took several centuries to complete and sparked increased study of the texts and the development of a group known as **scribes,** or rabbis (teachers).

The Cultural Situation

With most of the Israelites scattered and lost in foreign countries, the few who remained were desperately trying to hang on to their ways – their language, culture, law and religion. They knew that it was up to them and that if they forgot their history and language and God's promises, they would be gone forever.

> With most of the Israelites scattered and lost in foreign countries, the few who remained were desperately trying to hang on to their ways.

But maintaining their culture was not easy. When Alexander the Great began conquering the ancient world, he brought with him a "world culture" based on Greek philosophy, law and political administration. This was to have a huge impact on the Israelites in a number of ways. It may be hard for us to understand what it was like, but perhaps we can compare it to how in the modern world, many foreign cultures have been Americanised. The United States has a tremendous and overpowering influence. People in distant countries watch American movies and TV shows, listen to American music, drink Coke, wear baseball caps backward, eat hot dogs, wear American T-shirts, play basketball and know the tune of the American national anthem. They even say things like "What's up?" and "Peace out" and call each other "Dude!" And in a bizarre twist, many people around the globe know more about American history than they do about the history of their own country.

Back then, it wasn't the Americanisation of the world, it was the Hellenisation (Greek influence) of the world. Greek became the standard, universal language of the ancient world as Greek ways and customs flourished. Alexander actively encouraged the intermarriage of people of different backgrounds to water down cultural divisions. And most important, the Greeks were responsible for hummus, tabouli, vine leaves and souvlaki, which everyone knows are four of the best foodstuffs ever created. In fact, much of the Greek culture that developed in this period – architecture, art, literature, philosophy, science, government – still influences our world today.

This Greek way of life was everywhere and was seen by many as a threat to God's people, who were trying to preserve their own sense of culture and identity. Worst of all for many of the Jews was the religious idolatry that the Hellenistic culture brought with it. The idol worship and polytheism (multiple gods) that accompanied Greek life were in total opposition to God's commandments. The Romans, who had a whole swathe of deities, including the Roman emperor himself, continued this. The Romans were an advanced culture with huge military might and political structures. They had temples dedicated to many gods and, like the Greeks, a strong and dominant culture. Herod, the Roman-appointed (non-Jewish) king of Judea, rebuilt the temple in Jerusalem, starting in 20 BC. It was an enormous fifteen-storey structure that would dominate the Jerusalem of Jesus' day. (The Romans demolished it in AD 70.)

Waiting for a Deliverer

At the end of the Old Testament period, a movement of hope and expectation was growing within the Israelite community that a deliverer – the Messiah – would come and restore the kingdom to its former glory. Many believed that this Messiah, which translates as "the Anointed One", would overthrow the Romans and establish God's kingdom, vindicating Israel in the process. In fact, by the time we reach the pages of the New Testament, the dominant debate among the religious leaders of Israel was the *how*, *when* and *who* regarding the Messiah.

Their history and writings told them that their ancestors had been in similar hopeless situations before. They knew that God had raised a man – Moses – who led the people out of their desperate situation in Egypt. He was their deliverer, their rescuer. They knew that the judges had rescued and led the people in times of distress and military occupation. And now that this generation was in a similar situation, many people expected the same thing to happen. They expected a chosen one of God to rise up and rescue them again. This saviour would lead a rebellion, raise up a mighty army and overthrow the Roman government. It would be *pow! *%#@$#% bang! *&#$@%$^ +smash!* for the enemies of God; then the people would rebuild Israel to her former glory as a great and powerful nation. Many leaders did emerge during this time, and there were clashes and uprisings against the Romans. Many people lost their lives in battles or in punishment for their rebellion.

And God did send a special Saviour. About sixty years after the Roman Empire had taken over the known world, a baby was born in a backwater town. He would grow up to turn the world on its head and change the course of world history.

His name?

Jesus.

Jesus was God's Son who had come to live among us to restore once and for all the broken relationship between God and man. Throughout the Old Testament, many references are made to the expected arrival of this Chosen One.

> A movement of hope and expectation was growing that a deliverer – the Messiah – would come and restore the kingdom to its former glory.

But the Israelites didn't quite get what they expected. Yes, this man had come to save them. In fact, *Jesus* means "Saviour". His kingship was not about politics, however, and his rule was not about conventional war. He didn't come to save the Israelites from the Romans, but instead came to save them from their greatest enemy – sin. He came not to restore them to a mighty empire, but to restore them to a proper relationship with God.

And right there you have the whole point of the Bible. Here we go folks; this is where we get to the best part. The next few chapters describe what is undoubtedly the central and most important bit of the Bible.

Jesus is the heart of the entire Bible. He's the centre, the crux, the climax, the key point and the main event. From the beginning of Genesis, the entire Bible story builds to this event. And everything else you read in the Bible is because of it.

So let's not delay any longer. It's time to get into the New Testament.

The New Testament

Chapter 30

THE MAN FROM NAZARETH
The life of Jesus Christ
Matthew, Mark, Luke, John

Santa Claus arriving on a sleigh. A white Christmas. Shop windows spray painted with snow. Away in a manger. Sleighbells in the snow. Santa Claus conquers the Martians. Deck the halls.

Ah, yes, there's nothing quite like it. Each year, the biggest and most widely celebrated festival in the world is December 25, Christmas Day. It is a time when we say things like "Peace on Earth to All" and "Seasons Greetings". It is also a time when turkeys get nervous and retail stores make a squillion dollars.

While there are some who think that Christmas is the time when we worship the fat guy in the red suit from the North Pole, Christmas had much more humble beginnings. On Christmas Day, the world celebrates the single most important event in history: the birth of a child in a shed two thousand years ago. This long-awaited child was God's Son, the Christ. His parents named him *Jesus*.

People tend to have two pictures of Jesus. Either he is a cute baby in a crib surrounded by barnyard friends, or he is a hippy wearing a dressing gown going around ancient Palestine picking flowers, patting children on the head and telling everyone to love one another. The historical accounts of Jesus in the Bible, however, present a Jesus who was radical, appealing, powerful, confronting, controversial and amazing.

The first four books of the New Testament (commonly referred to as "the Gospels") give us a front-row view of the life of Jesus, as they record his birth, ministry, trial, execution and the amazing story of how he came back from death. Each of these books has its own distinct style as it narrates the story and teachings of Jesus, but all of them are united in presenting him as the Son of God, who is the great climax of all that has happened in the Bible so far.

One of the big ideas within the descriptions of Jesus' life is that of *fulfilment*. All that had been promised to the Israelites in the Old Testament, in some way or another, was fulfilled by, or in, Jesus. The prophets predicted where he would be born, that he would be born to a virgin, that he would do marvellous things, like restore the sight of the blind, proclaim good news to the poor and – in a reference to crucifixion – that he would be "pierced for our

> The historical accounts of Jesus in the Bible present a Jesus who was radical, appealing, powerful, confronting, controversial and amazing.

transgressions." In so many ways, Jesus fulfilled the words of the prophets who had spoken about him centuries before. He was the ultimate high priest, prophet and king. Bigger than Moses and David put together, more powerful than a locomotive and able to leap tall . . . um . . . he would rescue all people once and for all.

The way in which he brought about God's plans, however, was radically different from what many expected. The Israelites expected their nation to be restored by a military king, a deliverer like Moses, a king like David or a judge like Samson, who would rise up and kick out the foreign invaders, just like they used to in the good old days.

Instead, they got a "servant king" who was more interested in restoring their broken relationship with God. Instead of a military uprising, they got a spiritual uprising lead by Jesus. Jesus hung out with the lowest of the low in society, like prostitutes, tax collectors and authors; he challenged religious authorities; he performed amazing miracles; he out-argued the religious leaders; he went against the grain and taught controversial things, like "Love your enemies".

Matthew and Luke begin their accounts by narrating the miraculous circumstances of Jesus' conception and birth, born to a virgin named Mary. This remarkable event sets the scene for many more to come as all four gospels tell of Jesus' amazing adult life. Each gospel concentrates on the last three years of his life, beginning with his baptism by a bloke named John. This symbolic act of getting dunked in the Jordan River was seen as commissioning him for his role as the Saviour and King of the world. From then on, Jesus amassed a huge following as he preached, taught and performed many miracles. Crowds followed him wherever he went.

We (as in Ben and Pete) are big fans of U2, and when the band arrived in town for their first tour many years ago, Ben and some friends were desperate to meet Bono and the boys. Unfortunately, the hotel where U2 was staying was surrounded by hundreds of screaming fans. So Ben and his friends concocted a plan. They arrived at the hotel dressed in suits and ties and carrying briefcases to give the security guards the impression that they were hotel guests. They waltzed into the bistro for breakfast and, to cut a long story short, not only managed to meet the band but also grabbed a few autographs and photos as well.*

Jesus often found himself mobbed by "fans". People travelled into the desert to hear him speak. On one occasion, he had to escape the crowd by jumping into a boat. And as Ben did when trying to meet the members of U2, some people went to great lengths just to see Jesus. One guy climbed a tree so he could get a good view. Another group of enterprising men couldn't get near the packed building where Jesus was speaking, so they smashed a hole in the roof and lowered another friend through the hole on a rope!

*Ben, you're basically a big scammer!   —Pete

You're just jealous you didn't get to hang out with the guys from U2.   —Ben

Yes, that's true...but you're still a big scammer.   —Pete

Jesus was like an ancient rock star or celebrity. But rather than play huge power chords in a rock band or be the leading man in a feature film worthy of a dozen Oscars, Jesus ruled over nature as he calmed storms, turned water into wine, healed the sick and raised people from the dead. He ruled over evil as he cast out demons from people who were possessed. And most significantly, he ruled over sin as he forgave – as only God can forgive – those who turned to him in faith and humility. His miracles not only showed that he was powerful but that he was indeed Immanuel, "God with us". He was God in human form. When he calmed a storm and walked on the sea, he displayed control over nature, as God had done when the Israelites were escaping from the Egyptian army through the Red Sea. When he fed the five thousand, he did it in a manner similar to when God fed the Israelites in the wilderness on their journey to the Promised Land. And when he raised his friend Lazarus from the dead, Jesus showed that he was even Lord over life itself – something previously attributed only to God.

All the authors of the Gospels present a loving and accepting Jesus. He sat with notorious sinners and outcasts, eating with them and making them feel loved. The writers also make it clear, however, that he wasn't afraid to call a spade a shovel. He faced off against rulers and hotly spoke out against the notorious pride and arrogance of some of the religious leaders. He pulled no punches in confronting people and telling them to sort themselves out. He was a fiery preacher against sin.

Jesus spent most of his time with a particular group of twelve men who became his most loyal followers. These *disciples* accompanied Jesus from town to town and were constantly bewildered and amazed as they digested his words and watched his actions.

A large part of each gospel is devoted to Jesus' teachings, most of which come in the form of short stories (called *parables*) or debates with the religious leaders of the day. These words give us great insight into Jesus' life and teaching. His ultimate mission was not to make a million dollars and be really famous. His mission was to die and make it possible for us to be in relationship with God again. Many of his sayings and parables subtly revealed his identity and mission, which at times seemed to confuse his disciples. It was not until later that his followers fully understood who he was and what he came to do.

As Jesus' following and popularity increased, so did the opposition of some of the Jewish leaders. His words were sometimes controversial, and his teachings rubbed the pious religious leaders the wrong way. They thought he was sacrilegious and offensive. While thousands were gathering to hear him, a group of jealous Jewish religious leaders began to plan Jesus' downfall. This antagonism grew and headed toward a terrible climax. They wanted him out of the way for good. They wanted Jesus sleeping with the fishes. They wanted him dead.

Jesus' mission was to die and make it possible for us to be in relationship with God again.

About now you might be asking, why was there all this hostility toward Jesus? Surely he posed no threat to the religious leaders. The reason for their antagonism was that Jesus made himself equal with God. When a paralytic was brought to him on a stretcher in front of a large crowd, Jesus not only healed the man but also told him, "Your sins are forgiven." Everyone knew that only God could forgive sin. Little wonder, then, that the people ended up saying to one another, "Who is this man that forgives sins?" On another occasion, when Jesus was challenged by some of the religious leaders in a debate about his teachings, Jesus committed the ultimate sacrilege by claiming to be God. They were so incensed, they picked up rocks to stone him to death. He escaped their clutches on that occasion. A time would come, however, when he would fall right into their hands.

Where are we?

The life of Jesus is recorded in the first four books of the New Testament – Matthew, Mark, Luke and John. These books are commonly called "Gospels", a word meaning "great news" or "newsflash".

What time is it?

Matthew and Luke cover the same time span, about thirty-six years, from the conception and birth of both John the Baptist and Jesus until the resurrection of Jesus after his death. The majority of these two books' narratives, however, focus on the last three years of Jesus' life. Mark and John concentrate on Jesus' adult life after his baptism.

In a nutshell

All four gospels record the amazing life, death and resurrection of Jesus of Nazareth in their own distinctive way.

Who are the main people?

Jesus, Joseph and Mary, the twelve disciples, a broad range of people from all parts of society.

Miscellaneous

- Matthew was a tax collector. His gospel was placed first because it contained more references to the Old Testament than the other gospels.

- Luke is the longest book of the New Testament, and Luke chapter 1 is the longest chapter of the New Testament. Luke also wrote a sequel, the book of Acts.

- The first ever vocal radio broadcast was made on Christmas Eve 1906 in Brant Rock, Massachusetts. The Canadian-born Reginald Fessenden read out Luke chapter 2 and played a hymn on his violin.

- John 11:35 is the shortest verse in the New Testament.

- The plump, red-suited and white-bearded Santa Claus was created by the artist Haddon Sundblom in 1931 as part of an advertising campaign for Coca-Cola.

- "Christ" was not Jesus' surname but his title, meaning "Anointed One". He was Jesus, the Christ, meaning he was Jesus, the Saviour. Followers of Christ are called Christians, and the religion is referred to as Christianity. The Hebrew word for *Christ* is "Messiah".

- Jesus' date of birth is, in most countries, traditionally celebrated on December 25. The exact date of Jesus' birth, however, is uncertain. Some historians, for example, believe it was more likely in April or May. In Holland and Belgium, Christmas presents are exchanged on December 6, while in Russia, Christmas is traditionally celebrated on January 7. In Columbia, January 7 is a national holiday, commemorating the day that travellers from the East visited Jesus.

- While many people celebrate Christmas lunch over turkey and roast vegetables, in other parts of the world, popular Christmas dishes include casserole (Finland), pork with brown peas (Latvia), carp or goose (Germany), herring and brown peas (Sweden) and smoked mutton (Iceland).

- Legend has it that the Christmas tree was a German tradition started by a Christian missionary in AD 725.

- The name Santa Claus is a modification of "Saint Nikolaus" (Klaus), the Bishop of Myra. The name Kris Kringle comes from the German "Christkindl", meaning "Christ child".

- Popular belief is that Jesus was born in a stable. Not necessarily so. This is implied from the fact that his first cot was a makeshift one in the form of an animal's feeding trough. But he could have been born in a cave or under a tree. He may also have been born in a house, as it was common practise then to keep animals inside, in a lower room. Either way, his entry into the world was modest.

- Popular belief is that the newborn Jesus was visited by three wise men. In fact, it is likely that this event took place up to two years after his birth. In addition, these men were astrologers or magi (not wise men or kings), and there is no mention of how many there were. There could have been ten.

- No one knows what Jesus looked like, so any artistic or film depictions of him are pure imagination. Like the men of his region, he was probably about five feet tall and wore a beard and moustache. Considering his lifestyle, occupation and the harsh climate of the region, it is more likely that he was a brown and tough skinned nugget* rather than the lean, pasty intellectual of old Sunday school paintings. The common picture of the blue-eyed, beautiful Jesus came about in 1924, when illustrator Warner Sallman sketched a portrait of Jesus for a magazine. This picture has sold more than 500 million copies.

*Aussie Talk for a strong, robust, weathered person.

One of the recurring themes in the Old Testament is that disobeying God has serious consequences. It results in judgment and being cut off from God's blessings.

"Yeah, so what?" you may say. "I haven't sculpted any golden calves lately. Nor have I worshiped Baal. I haven't eaten from any tree that God told me not to. In fact, I've had a pretty good week all round!"

Sure, we may be "good" on one level. You may not litter, you pay your tax and hopefully you haven't killed anyone. But ultimately, we have little regard for God and his ways, and the bottom line is that each of us would rather be the ruler of our own lives. This means we have all disobeyed God and are not in a perfect relationship with him. None of us can be "good" enough to earn our way to God. This puts us in a serious dilemma. Our relationship with God is broken. The punishment is death. But we can't do anything by ourselves to fix it.

The sacrificial system (that we read about in the Old Testament) was designed to temporarily resolve this problem. An innocent animal could take the punishment for sin by being sacrificed in the place of the guilty. But people continued to sin, and sacrifices were continually needed.

The good news is that God deeply loves us and chose to solve our dilemma once and for all. A perfect sacrifice took our punishment – yours, mine, ours, everyone's – so we could be right again, once and forever, with God. And right there you have the central message of the Bible. Right there you have the message of Christianity. *Someone else took our punishment for ignoring God.*

Ben, the co-author of this book, is no stranger to having someone else take his punishment. When he was six years old, he nicked a biscuit from the kitchen, but finding it to be stale and disgusting, he threw it in the toilet. Thirty minutes later, Ben and his little sister were in big trouble, with Dad demanding to know who had put a biscuit in the toilet. Ben's theory that the neighbours must have flushed it down *their* toilet, and it had come up through the plumbing into the *Shaw* toilet did not go down well with his dad.

"Ben," he said in his most serious tone, "take your sister into your room and sort it out. If you two don't come out in five minutes with an answer, I'll cancel next week's family holiday."

> None of us can be "good" enough to earn our way to God.

Ben took his sister into the bedroom, closed the door and said, "Listen, one of us has to own up . . . I think *you* should." His sister thought about it for a moment and said, "Ok, I'll own up." Ben couldn't believe it!

They went out and Joanne owned up. Their father looked at her and said, "You've done wrong, and you know there are consequences." Joanne nodded while Ben stood there too gutless to say anything. Their Dad promptly marched her off to another room, where she was punished instead of Ben.

We know what you're thinking! You're thinking, *That wicked Ben Shaw! He should have his eyes gouged out, his arms ripped off, his hair pulled out.** The point of the story is that Joanne received Ben's punishment, and Ben got off scot-free. But even Joanne can't save us from our own broken relationship with God. The perfect sacrifice, who was killed in our place, was God's own Son, Jesus. Jesus stands before our Father in heaven, so to speak, and God looks at Jesus as the guilty and us as the innocent, even though it's the other way round. While Ben had to coerce his sister into taking the punishment for him, Jesus knew all along what was at stake and volunteered himself all the same. Jesus never sinned and was never out of relationship with God. He was the only truly innocent being able to accept the wrath of God on our behalf.

This is why Jesus, speaking of himself, said that he "did not come to be served, but to serve, and to give his life as a ransom for many" (Mark 10:45). Let's turn our attention to the events of Jesus' death.

Because it is so important, the narrative of all four gospels slows down to record the final days of Jesus' life and his death in all its dramatic detail.

Throughout Jesus' later years, the Jewish leaders were increasingly jealous and hostile toward him. They hatched a secret plot to get him out of the way, for good. On a Thursday night, Jesus had a final evening meal with his twelve companions. Christians refer to this as "the Last Supper". It wasn't just a farewell party for the sake of having a feed together. The disciples didn't even know this was going to be their last meal with Jesus. The meal, however, is highly significant in understanding what Jesus was about to do. It was no coincidence that these events took place at the same time that the Israelites celebrated the Passover meal.* Jesus was initiating a new Passover celebration. He was going to be the Passover Lamb once and for all so that the curse of death would pass over those who put their faith in him.

Jesus knew that he was soon to be betrayed, and the mood must have been sombre as he waited for what was coming his way. You are probably familiar with what happens next. Mel Gibson's popular film *The Passion of the Christ* begins at this point and then graphically portrays the horrific treatment of Jesus as he is betrayed, tortured, tried and eventually executed by the Romans. This film has done a lot to convey both Jesus' determination and the brutality and violence of crucifixion in a realistic light.

*That's certainly what I think, Ben, you scumbag! — Pete

The perfect sacrifice, who was killed in our place, was God's own Son, Jesus.

*You will remember that in the book of Exodus, the final plague on Egypt was the plague of death. The Israelites sacrificed an animal and placed its blood above their doors, and as a result, the curse of death passed over them.

160

After the meal, Jesus went with his mates to a nearby garden where he prayed. What terrible hours they must have been as he faced his betrayal and death.

It was there that Jesus was betrayed by Judas – one of his best mates – who led a large group of armed men and soldiers into the garden to arrest him. Jesus was taken away into custody and charged by the Jewish leaders with blasphemy and treason against Rome. The disciples fled the scene.

The Gospels then tell of the various trials Jesus endured. He was first tried by the Jewish legislative council (the **Sanhedrin**,) where he was questioned about his mission and teachings. The trial came to an abrupt end when Jesus confirmed that he was the Son of God. This "blasphemy" (insult to God) proved to be the final straw for Jesus' religious opponents. The council moved quickly to have Jesus executed. To do this legally, however, they needed the sentence to be passed by the governor of Judea, a man called Pontius Pilate.

When Pilate questioned Jesus, he found him to be innocent and didn't really want to have him executed, so instead he had him whipped, mocked and beaten. In a last minute effort to have Jesus released, Pilate proposed that the crowd decide his fate. In accordance with a custom of the day, one criminal in custody was set free during the celebration of the Passover. A notorious criminal named Barabbas was released at the request of the crowd, while Jesus, who was declared by Pilate to be innocent, remained condemned to die. This becomes a wonderful symbol of what Jesus had come to do for the entire world. He, the innocent, died; while we, the guilty, go free. The death sentence was carried out immediately.

At that time, there were no electric chairs or firing squads. Instead, the Romans had much more creative ways to kill criminals. They could be thrown into a pit of lions, or stoned or used as sport in the gladiators' arena. Then there was crucifixion, a particularly cruel form of execution.

The condemned person was literally nailed, arms outstretched, to a wooden pole with a crossbar, with large metal spikes driven through their wrists and ankles. The cross was then hoisted up into the air until the base dropped into a hole. The condemned man was left to hang in agony until his body weight crushed his lungs and he suffocated, all the while being gawked at by bystanders who looked on as if they were spectators at a football game.

Probably you have already noticed that the Christian faith has a lot to do with the cross. Walk into a traditional church building and you may see crosses on tables, walls, pews, Bibles and doors and windows. Many traditional church buildings were even built in the shape of a cross. Christians talk about the cross, sing songs about the cross and mention the cross in their services and prayers. Some Christians wear crosses around their necks, while others can be quite cross, especially if you talk in church when they're trying to listen. On

> He, the innocent, died; while we, the guilty, go free.

top of all that, odds are on that around Easter time, you have eaten a bun with a cross on it.

So what's the big deal about the cross?

When you think about it, it is actually quite bizarre and almost grotesque that Christians put a symbol of execution in their churches and around their necks as jewellery. You can hardly imagine having a gold-plated mini electric chair at the front of a church, or a noose hanging from a church steeple, or a lethal-syringe pendant. The cross itself has no mysterious power. Because it was where Jesus died, however, the cross has become a *symbol* of this most significant moment in world history.

On that Friday morning, Jesus was forced to carry a heavy wooden cross as he walked through the town gates. He was mocked, beaten and jeered at, then crucified between two other men. In one of the most touching scenes in the Bible, Luke tells us how one criminal asked Jesus to remember him when Jesus would "come into his kingdom". It seems, in complete irony, that a convicted criminal recognised Jesus' kingship when Jesus was at his weakest moment. Mark's gospel narrates a similar event. At the point when Jesus breathed his last breath, people heard a nearby Roman centurion utter, "Surely this man was the Son of God!" (Mark 15:39). What the disciples failed to fully grasp during the three years they were with Jesus was now plainly evident to a condemned criminal and a hardened Roman soldier. Here the Son of God was dying for the sins of the world, yet only a few grasped the significance of the event.

That Friday, Jesus died nailed to a pole in a most horrible way. His disciples had abandoned him, scattered and scared. Judas, racked with guilt because of his betrayal, tried to return the blood money to the priests and eventually committed suicide.

Jesus was removed from the cross and placed in a guarded tomb. The man who calmed the seas, healed the sick and spoke with tremendous authority, the man who turned the world on its head with his teaching, the man who was sent to save the world, was dead. There was no heroic music. No great battle. Just an ugly execution.

But this is not the end of the story.

The cross itself has no mysterious power. It has become a *symbol* of this most significant moment in world history.

Where are we?

The trial and death of Jesus is a major feature near the end of all four gospels. You can read about it in Matthew 26–27, Mark 14–15, Luke 22–23 and John 18–19.

What time is it?

There is some debate over precisely which year Jesus died, but most contemporary historians place his death in the year AD 33.

In a nutshell

The opposition to Jesus and his teaching reached its climax. Before Jesus was arrested and crucified, he had a final meal with his disciples. Jesus was then betrayed by Judas, arrested and tried before a number of different authorities. He was finally condemned to die on a cross. The Son of God died for all humanity.

Who are the main people?

Jesus, Caiaphas (the high priest), Barabbas, Pontius Pilate, the twelve disciples.

Miscellaneous

- Jesus was crucified at a place called Golgotha, which means "the place of the skull".

- In Christian church services, the last supper of Jesus is remembered. Christians eat a piece of bread and take a sip of wine or grape juice to remind them of Jesus and what he did. This ceremony is called communion or the Lord's Supper.

- In the epic movie *The Greatest Story Ever Told*, classic western actor John Wayne played the Roman centurion. Supposedly, when the director asked Wayne to put more "awe" into his speech, the actor said, "Awwwww, surely this man was the Son of God".

- The Friday before Easter (the day we remember Jesus' death) is known as "Good Friday". This seems an oddly upbeat name for such a horrible event. Yet it is called this because Jesus' death is such a "good" thing for us.

- Around the world, Jesus' death is commemorated in many different ways, generally reflecting local culture and history:
  - Religious processions and "passion plays" are popular in Latin America and some Asian nations. There have been incidents of people in the

Philippines voluntarily being crucified to commemorate Easter. They only are on the cross temporarily, but even so, the practise is discouraged.

- Festivities in Mexico involve the beating, hanging and burning of an effigy of Judas.

- People in Poland and Latin America throw water on each other and passers-by after Easter as a gesture of wishing good health.

- Other countries include rituals such as watching the sun rise (in remembrance of Christ's rising), foot-washing ceremonies and fireworks displays.

- The world's most famous Easter celebration is the passion play in Oberammergau, Germany. The play is performed every ten years with a cast of seventeen hundred locals taking part. This tradition began in 1634 as the villagers' vow of gratitude to God for sparing their village from the bubonic plague. There is seating for five thousand people, and tickets generally sell out many years in advance.

At the end of *Star Wars* episode 4, Obi-Wan Kenobi has a light-sabre fight with Darth Vader. He says to Vader, "If you strike me down, I will become more powerful than you can possibly imagine." Vader dispatches him with a deft blow of his light-sabre, and Obi-Wan dies.

But that wasn't the end of the story. It was just the beginning. Obi-Wan was right. He does become more powerful and actually comes back from death, popping back from time to time as a spirit or a voice, interacting with the other characters and helping to defeat the evil empire. You can't help but wonder if George Lucas based his fiction on the real-life events of Jesus.

Without stretching the point too far, the death of Jesus wasn't the end of the story either. Because it was through his death that Jesus showed his real power. What happened next revealed Jesus to be more powerful than you could possibly imagine. It was late on Friday afternoon when Jesus' body was removed from the cross and placed in a tomb belonging to Joseph of Arimathea. Due to concern that the disciples would take Jesus' body, some of the Jewish leaders obtained a Roman guard from Pontius Pilate for the tomb.

Early on the Sunday after Jesus' death, some women led by Mary Magdalene left Jerusalem to visit the tomb. They were not prepared for what they saw. The soldiers who were meant to be guarding the tomb were no longer there, the heavy entrance stone had been rolled to the side and Jesus' body was nowhere to be found. *Perhaps someone had stolen the body!* While they were standing there in disbelief, an angelic messenger told them that Jesus had indeed risen from the grave.

Meanwhile, the disciples were hiding in the upper room of a house, still in shock over the events of the past week. Their teacher and master – the one they thought was the Christ, the one who calmed storms, healed the sick and taught the masses – had not led them to glorious victory. Instead, he had become a convicted criminal who had been executed and buried. They were shattered.

After betraying Jesus and turning him over to the authorities, Judas had subsequently committed suicide in shame. Peter had on three occasions publicly denied that he ever knew Jesus. And the rest of the disciples had fled the

> It was through his death that Jesus showed his real power. What happened next revealed Jesus to be more powerful than you could possibly imagine.

scene at the time of his arrest. Now many of them met together again, confused, frightened and leaderless.

The women raced back to where the disciples were staying. No doubt the women's hearts were pounding from the wonder and excitement of it all. When they came to the disciples, they immediately told them what they had seen and learned. Understandably, most of the disciples didn't buy it. They laughed off the women's report as an idle tale and nonsense, or in today's language, "a bull story" (Luke 24:11). But at least two of the disciples paid the account enough respect to run to the tomb to check for themselves.

A short time later, the disciples' world was turned upside down again. While they were together in the room, Jesus came in and spoke to them. Understandably, the disciples were scared, thinking they were seeing a ghost. Jesus calmed their fears, telling them it was really he and then asking if he could have something to eat.

> The man on the cross had died, but now he was alive.

Think about this for a moment. The whole situation must have been awesome for the disciples as they watched Jesus, with the marks of his crucifixion still visible, walk around that room. The man on the cross had died, but now he was alive. And we're not talking about any operating-theatre story, when a person's heart stops for a minute and they see a white light at the end of a tunnel while a surgical team desperately smacks them with a defibrillator and they come back to life and then appear on Oprah. Jesus died a real death. He was dead for three days. We are talking stone-cold dead, efficiently executed by the military of a harsh and oppressive regime. And he came back to full life. Whereas our fictional Obi-Wan only ever appears as a shimmering hologram-type figure, Jesus returned in full flesh and blood.

This is the most amazing thing ever to happen on this planet. Someone had died, his life extinguished. He had journeyed into the great beyond after this life. (That in itself is not so amazing. After all, we all die.) Shakespeare referred to the afterlife in Hamlet as "the undiscover'd country from whose bourn no traveller returns". However, like a great explorer, Jesus did travel back. He did return, smashing the barrier between this physical world and the realm of the spirit. This coming back to life is referred to as the **resurrection.** This was a very, very, extra-very, super important event.

First, the resurrection of Jesus confirms that he was indeed the Christ and the one who was able to take the full weight of God's wrath on behalf of all humanity and also that his sacrifice was acceptable to God. It was the triumphant and climactic end to Jesus' time on earth. It showed to all that he was who he claimed to be and that he was Lord even over death.

Second, his resurrection paved the way for all those who trust in him to be raised to life as well. In a conversation with a friend, Jesus said, "I am the resurrection and the life. Anyone who believes in me will live, even though they die; and whoever lives by believing in me will never die" (John 11:25). This is the "good news" of the Bible.

The New Testament reports that Jesus appeared to more than five hundred of his followers on a number of other occasions, over a period of about forty days. It was during this time that Jesus showed the disciples how the whole of the Old Testament points to this moment. Shortly they too would tell the world of this new understanding (as described in the book of Acts), but for a brief moment in history, a few men and women sat at the feet of the resurrected Jesus and soaked up possibly the best sermon in history.

The final scene of Jesus' earthly life was his departure from the world as he headed off to be with God. At the beginning of the book of Acts (immediately following the Gospels), Jesus told the disciples that he must leave them, but they were to wait in Jerusalem for a gift. God would send the Holy Spirit, who would live with them and give them power to do amazing things as they spread the news about Jesus throughout the world. Jesus ascended into the sky in front of the awestruck disciples.

Although this marked the end of Jesus' life on earth, it was only the beginning of things to come. The disciples, armed with their good news about Jesus, would go on to change the world forever. Jesus had gone, but as he left, he said, "I'll be back".

> Jesus said, "I am the resurrection and the life. Anyone who believes in me will live, even though they die; and whoever lives by believing in me will never die."

Where are we?

We are at the end of each of the four gospels. The resurrection is described in Matthew 28, Mark 16, Luke 24 and John 20–21. The next book, Acts (written by Luke), is the historical sequel to the Gospels.

What time is it?

Jesus appeared to the disciples and many other people over forty days sometime in the year AD 33.

In a nutshell

Once Jesus had been executed and removed from the cross, he was placed in a guarded tomb. A number of women went to the tomb, only to find it empty. They told the disciples, who found the story a little farfetched. Jesus finally appeared to the disciples over a forty-day period, teaching them about his mission and God's purpose. He left the disciples with instructions to wait for the Holy Spirit, and then he ascended to heaven (Acts 1).

Who are the main people?

Jesus, Mary Magdalene and other women, the disciples.

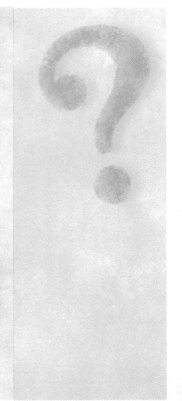

Miscellaneous

- According to historical tradition, almost all of the twelve apostles were eventually killed for their faith in Jesus and the belief that he rose from the dead.

- It is worth noting that women, not men, were the first to give an account of the risen Jesus. In the first century, women had no legal power as witnesses in a court of law. A woman's testimony was considered unacceptable. If the resurrection story was fabricated (as some may suggest), why would they have chosen the unacceptable testimony of women as the first witnesses?

- If someone doesn't believe something you say, you might call him or her "Doubting Thomas". This phrase comes from the fact that one of the disciples, Thomas, would not believe that Jesus had risen from death until he had seen him. Eventually, Jesus did appear to Thomas, and he stopped being a doubter.

- The world celebrates Jesus' death each year on Good Friday and his resurrection on the following Sunday, a day we call Easter. Amazingly, there is no mention of chocolate eggs or Easter bunnies in the Bible.

- Most countries have Easter celebrations related to eggs, which are a symbol of new life.

  - Many people exchange chocolate eggs at Easter, although in France, chocolate bells and fish are popular.

  - In Greece, Ukraine and Russia, eggs are painted bright red to symbolise Jesus' blood. It is common to play "conkers" with the eggs, along with the words "Christ is risen!" as a greeting, followed by the response "Truly, he has risen!"

  - In Russia, Easter-egg painting is considered an elaborate and valuable art form, with the intricate art techniques often handed down through generations. Some eggs become family heirlooms.

  - Easter-egg rolling is a popular tradition in the United States, England, Scotland and Germany. Each year, the American president hosts an Easter-egg hunt 'n' roll, involving thousands of people. It is the largest public event held at the White House, with activities planned for children age six and under.

Chapter 33

MEN WITH A MISSION
The start of the church
Acts

Scene:	*An upper room in a mud-brick building in ancient Palestine. Disciples sit in a circle, looking around expectantly. Suddenly Jesus appears in the middle of them.*
Jesus:	Good morning, disciples.
All:	AAAAAgggghhhh! IIIIiiiieeee!
Jesus:	Settle down. I told you I'd be back. Now, I have a mission for you. Go out into the world and preach the good news to all creation. Make disciples of all nations, baptising them and teaching them to obey everything I have commanded you. Any questions?
(Pause)	
Thomas:	Look, I don't want to be a wet rag or anything, but we're just a bunch of simple guys. How are we supposed to go out into the world and do anything? No offence Jesus, but you died and now you've come back, and I'm still a bit freaked out.
Peter:	You're such a doubter, Thomas!
Thomas:	Well, we're not exactly the most popular guys at the moment. The Romans and everyone else are looking at us kind of funny and, well, even Peter denied that he knew –
Peter:	Oh, you had to bring that up!
Thomas:	And look what happened to Judas.
Peter:	Serves him right, that dirty old –
James:	Cut it out, you two. Jesus, Thomas is right. We are just fishermen. It was okay when you were here, but who are *we* to go out and . . . *(checking his notes)* what was it you said? . . . "make disciples of all nations"? We're just not equipped for the mission!
Jesus:	Have no fear, my friends. Wait here in Jerusalem for a gift from God. He will equip you with the Holy Spirit, a powerful companion who will be with you.

(Disciples look at each other)

Simon the Zealot:	Um ... (*awkwardly*) I think James was talking more about some cool stuff like infrared sunglasses and satellite phones ...
Andrew:	... and sports cars with missiles ...
Jesus:	Enough!
(Awkward silence)	
James:	How will we know when the gift arrives?
Jesus:	Um, let's see. The sound of a mighty wind, tongues of flame ... Trust me. You won't miss it.
(Disciples nod)	
Jesus:	I won't lie to you. It is a difficult mission. Some would even say a mission impossible. Your lives will be in grave danger. This is your mission, should you choose to accept it.
All:	We accept!
Jesus:	Good. This message will self-destruct in ten seconds ...

> God's Holy Spirit transformed them from a frightened and confused bunch of followers hiding from the crowds to a bold and courageous team of witnesses.

Little did the disciples know that they were about to embark on tremendous adventures and play a critical part in the biggest phenomenon the world has ever seen. They would go on to spread the word about Jesus and start the Christian church.

The book of Acts begins with the small band of Jesus' followers being totally transformed in their understanding of who Jesus really was and what he came to do. At first they were devastated by the loss of their leader, petrified of the Roman government and dismayed that all their hopes that Jesus would be the great rescuer had come to nothing. All hope seemed lost. But when Jesus appeared to them a few days after his death, they knew that the party was far from over. In fact, it was just beginning.

A short while later, God's Holy Spirit came upon his followers in spectacular fashion. His Spirit transformed them from a frightened and confused bunch of followers hiding from the crowds to a bold and courageous team of witnesses. They became determined, strong and enthusiastic about their new mission. As promised, God had equipped them to do the job.*

The book of Acts tells of the trials and triumphs of the first Christians as they moved around the ancient world, telling others about the significance of Jesus and his death and resurrection. They started preaching and teaching in Jerusalem and Judea, and then they headed out into further regions, eventually spreading the good news of Jesus to all nations. There were mass conversions as people embraced the message of Jesus.

Acts largely records the travels and preaching of the apostle Paul. Originally named Saul, he was a zealous Jew who persecuted Christians for their faith, even overseeing the deaths of some of them. But Paul was powerfully transformed when Jesus appeared to him while he was travelling to Damascus.

*The disciples are sometimes referred to as apostles, which means "sent ones", or in colloquial language, "men with a mission".

No longer the active enemy of Jesus, Paul would become one of the most influential Christians in history.

The rest of Acts could be titled "The Adventures of the Apostle Paul", as it mainly records Paul's missionary trips throughout the Roman Empire. At times, things are tough for him and his mates as they are thrown in jail, chased out of towns, beaten, stoned and shipwrecked; yet on other occasions, things couldn't be better as they see people come to know the love of God through the disciples' preaching about Jesus Christ. The book of Acts is a great insight into the background of many of Paul's letters (which follow Acts) to the first churches and the issues facing them.

Where are we?

Acts comes right after the four gospels in the New Testament. Written to Theophilus as a historical account, Acts is a sequel to Luke's gospel.

What time is it?

Acts begins with Christ's resurrection and covers a period of almost thirty years, concluding with Paul in Rome. These events span the years AD 33–62.

In a nutshell

Acts tells how, through the lives and witness of the apostles – most particularly the apostle Paul – Christianity was to spread throughout the known world.

Who are the main people?

Peter, John, James, Phillip, Stephen, Paul, Barnabas.

Miscellaneous

- The book of Acts was written by Luke, who was probably a doctor.

- The oldest fragment of the book of Acts is kept at Macquarie University in Sydney. (Ben has held it!)

- The word *apostle* means "sent one" or "messenger". It refers to the twelve blokes who Jesus sent out to spread the message of the gospel. As such, the full name of the book is "The Acts of the Apostles".

- Paul was a Pharisee, but he also learned the trade of a tentmaker.

Chapter 34

YOURS SINCERELY, PAUL
The letters of Paul to the first Christians
Romans, 1 Corinthians, 2 Corinthians, Galatians, Ephesians, Philippians, Colossians, 1 Thessalonians, 2 Thessalonians, 1 Timothy, 2 Timothy, Titus, Philemon

Peter, John and Paul certainly did a good job in their missionary journeys (which we covered in the previous chapter, on the Acts of the Apostles). People heard the good news about Jesus and joined together to form groups with other new followers of Christ, or "Christ-ians". Church communities sprang up everywhere around the known world.

Back in these early days of Christianity, the church had no established infrastructure. There were no buildings called "St. Somebody's". There were no denominations. And while the church is considered conservative and "establishment" today, back then it was more of a radical movement. In fact, it even had a cool underground sort of name. People referred to it as **The Way.**

What comes to mind when you read the word *church*? A traditional building with stained-glass windows and a steeple? Pews, altars, morning-tea rosters and a big organ blasting out a hymn? There was none of that back then. The first Christians gathered together in homes. They were loosely identified by the city in which they lived. So when Paul wrote letters "to the church of God in Corinth" (1 and 2 Corinthians), the mail did not go to a bishop sitting in a cathedral in the Corinth town square. Rather, it was a group letter addressed to the Christians living and meeting together in that city.

These first Christians had lots of issues and questions, and even some misconceptions that needed sorting out. *So how do we live as followers of Jesus? How does Jesus' death save us? Why is it important that Jesus rose from the dead? Is salvation available to everyone or just the Jews alone? Are the old religious rites (like circumcision) still important? How should Christian husbands and wives treat each other? Why are people hassling me for my beliefs? What should be my attitude regarding money, slavery, leadership, sexuality, sin, marriage, the law, freedom and forgiveness? How should we cope with divisions and disagreements? When is Jesus coming back?*

Of course, today you can get information anywhere. You can get a Bible (or thousands of books) in any bookshop, or watch Christian films and TV shows, or chat with your local Christian minister, or surf the Net for millions of pages of information about Christianity. But information wasn't so readily available back then.

Way before Ben sat down with Pete to write this book, Ben played in a band that travelled extensively around the country and overseas. The band spent months on the road, playing and speaking to people in pubs, churches, festivals and even prisons. When they moved on to play elsewhere, they wanted to keep in contact with the friends they'd made along the way. Also, many people they spoke with wanted to ask them more questions about their faith and about Christianity in general. So once a week Ben and the other band members would sit down together and write letters to their newfound friends to catch up and to give them some friendly guidance and encouragement. On one occasion, Ben even had to write to a young bloke in prison to encourage him to keep reading his Bible even though other inmates were threatening to beat him up because of it.

The early Christians also needed guidance and encouragement and someone to teach them about what it meant to follow Jesus. So while the apostles travelled extensively around the Mediterranean region, they also wrote a lot of letters to the various church communities that had sprung up in the larger urban centres, generally in relation to issues and problems among the followers. These letters, although specific at one level, contain principles that are universal and timeless, even for us today.

Twenty-one of these letters, or *epistles* make up most of the New Testament. Paul wrote thirteen of them. Most of the letters were written to an entire church, designed to be read to the congregation: for example, Ephesians was a letter to the church in the trade city of Ephesus, where Paul had based himself earlier for more than two years. Some letters, however, were written to a church leader. So, 1 Timothy was a letter of direction and encouragement to Tim, one of Paul's mates, who was leading the Ephesian church.

Paul covers hundreds of topics in his letters. Many have to do with the significance of Jesus' death and resurrection. He explains how people are "saved" from their broken relationship with God when they put their faith in Jesus.

One of Paul's most significant themes in his letters is *grace.* He explains in various ways that people can get back into a right relationship with God purely because of the generosity or favour of God and for no other reason. A sinner is saved not because of his or her own merit but because of God's grace. Many Jews in Paul's day (and afterward) assumed they were automatically saved simply because they were Jews. Others thought they could get right with God by following the law to the letter or by performing rituals. But Paul argued that salvation was the result of God's grace alone.

Paul also addressed issues related to **Christian living.** He wrote about everyday matters, such as marriage, giving, working, prayer, money, immorality, dealing with lawsuits and what should happen in church. Many of these letters have formed the foundation of the Christian faith and church practise of the last two thousand years. To say nothing of 1 Corinthians 13:4–13, which has appeared in virtually every marriage service you've ever been to.

The early Christians needed guidance and someone to teach them about what it meant to follow Jesus.

A sinner is saved not because of his or her own merit but because of God's grace.

Where are we?

After the Gospels and Acts, the next twenty-one books are letters written to the first Christians. The first thirteen letters (Romans to Philemon) were penned by the apostle Paul.

What time is it?

Paul's letters were written from about the 40s to the 60s during the first century.

In a nutshell

The thirteen letters of Paul were written to the Christians of the early church to explain the significance of Christ's death and resurrection, how to live as a Christian and how the church should function.

Who are the main people?

Paul, the first Christians, some of Paul's closest friends, such as Timothy and Philemon.

Miscellaneous

- Paul was originally a Pharisee (a group of religious Jews who were very particular about following the law). He was extremely hostile to Christians until he became a Christian. Saul was his Jewish name, but he preferred Paul, his Greek name. You can read about his conversion in Acts chapter 9.

- Several of Paul's letters were written from prison.

- According to some non-biblical sources, Paul was beheaded in Rome because of his Christian faith.

- The only successful twentieth-century rock group mentioned in the Bible is found in Romans 8:15.

Chapter 35

INSTRUCTIONS FOR THE FAITHFUL
The General Letters
Hebrews, James, 1 Peter, 2 Peter, 1 John, 2 John, 3 John, Jude

I t's not always easy being a Christian in today's world.

Your family might not understand. Your neighbours might think you are silly for going to church. Your friends might think Christianity is for weirdos. The people you work with might say that Christianity is an outdated religion for people with their heads in the sand. Some people might poke fun at you for what you believe. Ben and Pete, for example, were both called a few names by their "mates" at high school because they went to church – names like drongo,* dork, wuss,** goody-goody, Bible basher and an assortment of names questioning their sexuality or intelligence, which cannot be printed in this book.

But no matter what hardships you have to suffer for being a Christian, it is likely they are chicken feed compared to what many early Christians experienced.

Throughout the centuries, Christians have been mocked, ridiculed, laughed at, persecuted, imprisoned, tortured, discriminated against and killed for their Christian belief.

In the first century, the Roman emperor Nero had Christians sewn into bags made of animal skins, then chased and killed by packs of dogs. On another occasion, he soaked some Christians in wax, fixed them to axletrees and used them as human torches to light up his garden. Christians were also sometimes used as public entertainment in the arena as fodder for wild animals or gladiators. They had property and possessions taken from them and lost their legal rights. According to tradition, most of the apostles were killed because of their faith. It is believed that both Paul (who wrote most of the New Testament) and Peter were killed sometime in the late 60s of the first century. Paul was beheaded, and Peter was crucified upside down. It certainly was dark days for those first Christians.

Little wonder that they needed encouraging! These eight letters were written during the troubled and hostile times of the first century AD to encourage Christians to hold on to their beliefs and lifestyle. Some of those early Christians were struggling to live out their faith in places where they might be ridiculed or even killed for it. Some were questioning the greatness of Jesus,

*Aussie talk for "stupid, inept, awkward, embarrassing".
**Aussie talk for "coward" or "weakling".

> Throughout the centuries, Christians have been mocked, ridiculed, laughed at, persecuted, imprisoned, tortured, discriminated against and killed for their Christian belief.

These letters were written to give Christians confidence that Jesus was truly the promised Messiah, to encourage the believers to hang in there through the dark times and to encourage them to live and breathe a life that was pleasing and right to God.

while others were thinking about giving up their faith altogether and going back to their former ways. Some were struggling with the ramblings of bad teachers, while others were starting to get into things that weren't necessarily good for them. These letters were written to give Christians confidence that Jesus was truly the promised Messiah, to encourage the believers to hang in there through the dark times and to encourage them to live and breathe a life that was pleasing and right to God.

These writings have been called "the General Letters" since the fourth century because of their general audience and broad topics. Like Paul's letters, these cover a wide variety of topics and explain the benefits of following Jesus. They are highly informative, encouraging, and at times, heart warming. At the same time, they are hostile toward bad teachers and bad teaching.

Even today, it is illegal in some countries to become a Christian, and the penalties are harsh. Christians are still persecuted, put in jail or killed for their beliefs. Although these letters were written about two thousand years ago, they still apply to situations today and remain a great source of encouragement to Christian people in times of darkness and doubt.

Where are we?

The General Letters come immediately after Paul's church letters (Romans to 2 Thessalonians) and personal pastoral letters (1 Timothy to Philemon) and before the final book of the Bible, Revelation. (We're almost there, folks!)

What time is it?

These letters were written at different times between the 60s and 90s of the first century AD.

In a nutshell

These eight letters were written by a number of authors (James, Peter, John, Jude) to Christians who needed teaching, encouraging or correcting. They cover a multitude of topics, from the supremacy of Christ to a definition of faith and the social behaviour of believers.

Who are the main people?

James, Peter, Jude, John, various friends, churches and leaders.

Miscellaneous

- The author of Hebrews is unknown.

- James was one of Jesus' brothers.

- Second John is only thirteen verses long and is the shortest book in the Bible.

- These General Epistles used to be called "the Catholic Letters" because of their universal nature. The word *catholic* means "universal".

Chapter 36

SEEING BEYOND
What does the future hold?
Revelation

I magine you are in a movie theatre, mouth full of popcorn and busting to go to the toilet.

You are watching a special-effects extravaganza. A spiritual hero with white hair like blazing fire and seven stars in his right hand; a throne encircled by twenty-four other thrones, sending out peals of lightning and thunder; there is a great earthquake, the sun turns black and the moon turns blood red; the trumpet sounds, and hail and fire rain down on the earth; multi-headed beasts rise up; living creatures die, great ships are destroyed, locusts sweep across the earth; 200 million troops sweep forward on horses breathing fire, smoke and sulphur – it is a mighty battle, the final confrontation between good and evil.

You would be excused for thinking you were watching something written by J. R. R. Tolkien, starring a Hollywood action hero. But no. This is the book of Revelation. The final book of the Bible is perhaps the most enthralling and controversial of all the books. It certainly reads differently than any other New Testament book. It has been the source – often vaguely and incorrectly – of the inspiration and images behind scores of horror novels and multitudes of Hollywood films, like *End of Days*, *The Seventh Seal* and *The Omen* series. The number of the beast (666), the final judgment day and a description of heaven are all located within this book and are the daily bread of heavy-metal lyrics and horror films.

It should come as no surprise that the book of Revelation has caused much confusion. Many cults and strange beliefs have come from incorrect interpretations of several of the passages within it. The key to understanding Revelation is to understand the type of literature it is.

In 1945, George Orwell released a now classic novel called *Animal Farm*. In the book, a group of pigs rise up and lead a rebellion against the oppressive farmers. The animals – horses, cows, chickens, sheep – take over the farm and have various adventures. On the surface, it is just an animal story. But in fact, the novel is **symbolic,** actually telling the story of the Russian Revolution. The animal farm is the Soviet Union, and the farmhouse is the Kremlin. The pig Snowball represents Trotsky, while the pig Napoleon represents Stalin, and his

> The final book of the Bible is perhaps the most enthralling and controversial of all the books.

dogs are the KGB. Nearby Foxwood Farm is England, while Pinchfield is Germany. The novel is a metaphor, with each character and event representing something or someone in the real world.

Much of the book of Revelation is written in a similar symbolic style and is not meant to be taken literally. A number of writers in the ancient world used this style to describe both physical and spiritual events.

The book of Revelation is like a group email; it is a letter the apostle John wrote to seven churches in Asia Minor while he was in prison on the tiny Roman penal-colony island of Patmos in the Aegean Sea. He wrote it at a time of growing hostility toward Christian people. Worship of the Roman emperor as a god was becoming common. John had been imprisoned because of his faith. Many others had been executed, and the young churches were heading for dark days of persecution and opposition.

So John wrote this letter to both warn and encourage the believers about what God was going to do in the future. Many scholars believe that much of this letter contains "apocalyptic literature", which symbolically describes events that were about to happen in the first century. For example, the lampstands are the churches, and the beast that comes out of the sea (Revelation 13) is not literally a bloke with horns growing out of his head but more likely a reference to imperial Roman power – a huge and imposing force in John's day.

Other parts of this book, however, undoubtedly describe events that are yet to occur. The final chapters preview the end of all time and are a fitting end not only to the letter but to the entire Bible. John describes the final days, when God's plans will be completely fulfilled. These final chapters paint a picture of heaven and the fully restored relationship between God and the human race, something that God has been trying to sort out since we stuffed things up back in Eden.

Judgment on all evil is graphically described. In a final fulfilment of the promise of the tabernacle, God will live at last with his people without sin getting in the way. Jesus (referred to as "the Lamb") will rightfully rule over all who have honoured him, on a new earth where there is no more suffering, pain or death. This is a climactic window into the end of time and the benefits of the death and resurrection of Jesus. This book was, and still is, a great source of encouragement and inspiration to Christians throughout the world.

These final chapters paint a picture of heaven and the fully restored relationship between God and the human race.

Where are we?

This is the last of the twenty-one letters in the New Testament, the final book of the New Testament and the final book of the Bible. (Congratulations. You made it!)

What time is it?

Historians have found it hard to reach a unanimous decision on the date when this book was written. It is safe to say that it was one of the last books of the New Testament to be written and was most likely penned sometime in the period between AD 60 and AD 90.

In a nutshell

The apostle John wrote the book of Revelation to seven churches in Asia Minor. Using symbolic language, the author teaches and encourages his audience by describing the events of both the near and far future. Chiefly, he writes of the greatness of God and how God plans to bring justice to his enemies and new life to his people.

Who are the main people?

Symbolically, the book describes a number of possible rulers or emperors (Nero, Domitian or Trajan). Jesus, of course, is the main star of the book and is described symbolically as "the Lamb", "the Alpha and the Omega" and "the bright Morning Star".

Miscellaneous

- The seven churches – Pergamum, Thyatira, Sardis, Smyrna, Philadelphia, Ephesus, Laodicea – were all in a 200-kilometre region in what is now Turkey. Of these, Ephesus was the only one that had one of Paul's letters to them published in the Bible (Ephesians).

- Revelation 20:4 is the longest verse in the New Testament.

- Revelation contains quotations from thirty-two Old Testament books, which is more than any other New Testament book.

STUFF AT THE BACK

The epigraph of this book was a traditional Christian children's ditty, and as Elvis said, it goes a little like this:

> The best book to read is the Bible.
> The best book to read is the Bible.
> If you read it every day,
> It will help you on your way.
> The best book to read is the Bible.

While being the kind of sweet and annoying song that makes you want to smash your twelve-string guitar and kick over a drum kit in front of a church full of old ladies, it does actually contain three significant truths; namely, the Bible is a great book to read (really, the best) and ultimately is far more important and meaningful than any other book; it should be read and consumed and thought about regularly (every day); and it has a lot to say to you that will have a deep impact on your life, attitudes, words, actions and decisions as it "helps you on your way".

But the question is, ***how do you read the Bible?*** You pick up the Bible and … *What then? How do I read this? Where to begin?*

Glad you asked. There are a number of different approaches people take when reading the Bible. Here are a few.

The Cover-to-Cover Method

When Ben first became a Christian, he decided that he was going to read the entire Bible from cover to cover, page by page as you would read a novel.

Things went well through Genesis, which was pretty straightforward. Exodus also was okay, although he found the going pretty tough after chapter 26 when it got into complex architectural details of the building of the tabernacle. Things really slowed down, however, when he hit the long lists and intricacies of Numbers. His grand plan eventually ground to a halt.

While it is certainly worthwhile reading the Bible from cover to cover (at the very least so you can impress your friends), this might not be the best option for the person starting out on his or her Bible journey. Reading the

Bible from cover to cover makes a lot more sense if you have an overview of the component parts and are familiar with many of the books. Walk before you run.

The Random-Selection Method

When Pete first became a Christian, he too wanted to read the Bible. He also decided that each night, half an hour before bed, he would sit at his desk and read a section. He developed a highly technical method that involved holding the Bible on its spine on the desk, closing his eyes, letting the Bible fall open and then placing his finger randomly somewhere on the page. He started to read from that point on, figuring that over time this would ensure a nice variety of biblical reading experiences. (Pete's intelligence developed later in life.)

One day he would read something like, "Your teeth are like a flock of sheep coming up from the washing. Each has its twin, not one of them is missing" (Songs 6:6). The next, "Then I looked, and there before me was the Lamb, standing on Mount Zion, and with him 144,000 who had his name and his Father's name written on their foreheads" (Revelation 14:1). And the next, "The whole company numbered 42,360, besides their 7,337 male and female slaves; and they also had 245 male and female singers. There were 736 horses, 245 mules, 435 camels and 6,720 donkeys" (Nehemiah 7:66–69).

While interesting, the problem was Pete didn't know what he was reading or how it fit with the rest of anything else. His reading had no continuity from day to day, and in short it was a nonsensical exercise. Please don't use this method.

The Insomnia Method

Another unsuccessful method is the old "I'll read the Bible as I sit here in bed just before I go off to sleep" method. This never works. The end of the day, when you are running on fumes, is not when your concentration is at its premium.

Sure, you start off sitting up and reading, but then you slowly slide down under the covers where it's nice and warm, and soon you are asleep with your Bible closed on your head and you are dribbling on the pages and you wake up the next morning with an imprint of 2 Chronicles 12 on the side of your face. Don't use this method either.

The Shopping-Cart Method

Some people treat the Bible like a supermarket.

Its "shelves" are filled with a huge variety of verses and statements and phrases and words, and you simply wander through the aisles, picking out the bits you like and popping them into your cart. You can grab a verse from *here* and a paragraph from *there* and put them together to say whatever you like. You end up with a fast-food handle on the Bible, as if it is some sort of feel-good desk calendar filled with thousands of inspirational titbits and sayings like "He who spares the rod hates his son", and "All come from dust, and to dust return", and "Love is patient, love is kind. It does not envy, it does not boast, it is not proud".

You end up with a bitsy perception of the Bible, lacking in overall meaning, theme, structure or continuity. Ultimately, it makes no sense and your reading serves no purpose.

The Instantaneous-Bible-Expert Method

This is Pete's "failed Bible reading method no. 2".

As a young Christian, Pete bought a book called *Search the Scriptures*. This is a systematic study program, and by reading just twenty minutes a day, you can cover the entire Bible in three years.

Overcome with the zealousness of youth, Pete decided that three years was far too long. He wanted to get up to speed a lot quicker and calculated that if he did three times as much as *STS* suggested, he could finish the whole Bible in one year instead of three. He lasted about three weeks before burning out. The Bible has a lifetime of stuff to encounter. You don't have to read it all at once!

There is something to be said for being patient and remembering that slow and steady wins the race.

Enough stories about how *not* to read the Bible.

How *Do* You Read the Bible?

Here are a few principles that may aid you in your Bible-reading adventures.

The first thing to say is that if you are a Christian person, it is important to read the Bible. This is the same sort of understatement as "If you are a human, it is important to breathe".

Ben and Pete both play the guitar. In fact, they both play the guitar pretty well.*

They got good at playing the guitar by playing it every day over years and years. This is the same with the Christian and the Bible. You get good at knowing the Bible and learning from it by spending time reading it over a long period of time.

It isn't enough just to hear passages read out loud in church once a week. This would be like trying to learn to play the guitar by watching a music-video clip on television once a week. It would not come to much. You have to get into it yourself.

Reading the Bible teaches you about history and God and who he is and what it means to live your life as a Christian. It tells you stuff for your head and stuff for your heart. It is an important book! It shapes your life and influences your decisions, relationships and attitudes. It strengthens your understanding about God and being a Christian.

> The first thing to say is that if you are a Christian person, it is important to read the Bible.

*Pete actually plays the guitar better than I do.
– Ben

C'mon Ben, we both know you play guitar better than me. – Pete

Oh no, I . . . well, actually . . . now that I think about it, you're right!
– Ben

Read your Bible!

Read your Bible!

This is important, so we'll say it again.

Read your Bible!

The next thing to say is that the Bible stands on its own. God reveals stuff to us through the Bible. You can actually read it and study it in isolation and make sense of what is going on in its pages without resorting to other sources. You don't need other books (like this one) to read the Bible.

But if you are new to the Bible, it's sometimes hard to know exactly where to start. If you were to ask a Christian person which five books the new Bible reader should read, you would get a lot of different answers, depending on people's tastes and experiences.

And so, for what it's worth, here's a possible list (note: not *the* list!) of some books of the Bible that would be a good place to start.

Maybe you can kick off with two gospels, say, the books of Mark and John. After that, go back and read the book of Genesis and the first twenty chapters of Exodus.

Then for a bit of variety, check out the book of Psalms. Probably not all of the chapters (too much for a first encounter), so read . . . um . . . well . . . say, Psalms 86, 96, 71, 89, 62, 33, 103, 77, 116, 113, 139, 57 and 145. They're pretty good. To finish off, zip back up to the New Testament to one of Paul's letters. The book of Philippians would be a good introduction to the letters of the New Testament. That'll do for starters.

Having said that the Bible stands on its own feet, many Christians find a study-guide book useful to direct their reading. Such guides encourage systematic and regular reading patterns. It's easier to cover a book or theme when there is order to your reading.

There are literally thousands of Bible study guides that can help you have a better understanding of what you are reading, provide information and pose questions about various issues. You can find them at your local Christian bookshop or in any of a squillion Bible study guide websites.

Study guides are available for any reading or knowledge level, from quite simple and easy guides for the person who is just starting out reading the Bible to highly complex and bulky guides for people who are after more meat in their Bible diet.

Some guidebooks explore issues or themes that run through a number of books. For example, prayer, marriage, attitudes to money, leadership or what it means to live as a Christian. Other guidebooks walk you through a single book, like Jonah or Revelation or any one of the other books of the Bible.

The final thing we want to say is that the Bible is like a bath. If you're going to have a bath, there's not much point just leaping in and leaping out again. You want to sink into it. Stay for a while. Soak.

We live in an age of high-speed information and communication. We scan the morning paper quickly for the main stories. We send quick SMS messages and fire emails back and forth like gunfire. Everything is snappy. Quick. Pow. Bang. Zap. Over and out. No time to sit and think. Badda Boom. Let's do lunch. Gotta keep moving. Bing.

You can't read the Bible in this frantic way. It's not something you flick your eyes over while you're chugging down your cereal before you rush out the door. You don't "grab a bite of the Bible" like you "grab a bite to eat". Rather, savour it like a three-course meal.

In a nutshell, what we are saying is that to get the most out of the Bible, don't just flick your eyes across the words. Rather, *read* them. Pause. Stop. Sit. *Think* about what you are reading. Contemplate. *Meditate.* Stew and ruminate. Masticate the words. Take your time. You may find it useful to keep a logbook or journal of your reading, so you can jot down ideas, comments and questions to explore further. Even better, you may find it helpful to read the Bible with a friend or a group, so you can discuss issues and ask questions.

When you read Jesus' and Paul's words about God's amazing grace and forgiveness (Luke 15, Colossians 1:19–22), or James's writings about being careful in what you say (James 3:1–12), or of the search for the meaning of human life (Ecclesiastes), or of the resolve of Shadrach, Meschach and Abednago (Daniel 3), or of Jesus' challenge to love others selflessly (John 13:34–35), give yourself time to think about what you have read. Think about what it means. How it affects you. Pray to God about the things you read and ask him to help you to understand his words more clearly so that they have a real impact on your life.

In short, let God speak to you through the words of his wonderful book!

Well, that pretty well wraps it up for us. But while our journey together in this book is coming to an end, hopefully you are about to embark on another journey that will ultimately be much more meaty and fulfilling – your own journey into the Bible.

You will recall that earlier we suggested that this book is like a travel guide that gets you ready for your travels in a foreign country.

Well, now you've read the guidebook. You've arrived at the Bible airport and are through Old Testament customs and have your New Testament traveller's cheques! The door is open before you, and it is time for you to step out into the exciting and life-changing world of Bible land.

Go on . . . off you go! No point hanging around here any more. The food in this airport is terrible!

Reach for your Bible and get into it.

Best wishes in your travels. We pray that God will bless you in your reading of his Word and that it will change your life forever!

Ben Shaw
Pete Downey

> In short, let God speak to you through the words of his wonderful book!

W e wanted to finish this book on a personal note. So we asked a bunch of people of various ages and backgrounds to give us a few words about a part of the Bible that is particularly relevant or meaningful to them.

Some chose a single verse or a passage, while others nominated an entire chapter or book. Many complained that it was unfair to ask them to single out just one part of the Bible. Of course, you can read about many great people and events and teachings in the Bible, and this list is just a minuscule selection. If we asked another group what they thought, we would no doubt get a totally different list of references. So in no way is this supposed to represent an exhaustive list. Nor is it designed to point you to "the best bits of the Bible" or anything like that. It's just to give you a flavour of a range of Bible excerpts and various people's reactions to them. Here's what they had to say.

Adele, 46, schoolteacher

2 Samuel 11 and 12

King David is one of the great men of God in the Bible. He was popular and famous. Yet even he sinned and did wrong. Reading about him sleeping with another man's wife and then trying to cover his tracks by committing murder is like reading the intrigue of a good crime novel. It always has me on the edge of my seat. I love the way Nathan traps David into realising the seriousness of what he has done. I am encouraged that even this great man of God struggled with life. It lets me know that I am not alone when I do wrong and that I can seek forgiveness in God.

Cameron, 25, legal clerk

Hebrews 4:12–13

Since I became a Christian back at the beginning of my high school days, I have had an interest in the Bible and learning about God. There are two key aspects of the Bible that interest me. The Bible specifically informs us how we have turned from God and the way we can get right with God. It also provides instructions on living our lives and resolutions for problems that we all face. One of my favourite passages in the Bible is this passage in

Hebrews, as these verses challenge me to think about how I act and what I do every minute of each day.

Deborah, 29, wife and full-time mother of three children
Romans 7:15–25

This passage is from a letter written by Paul to people in the church in Rome. In it he talks about the terrible predicament of wanting to do what is right but often finding himself doing the wrong thing. It reminds me that Jesus knows that I am human and that I make mistakes even though I endeavour to do the right thing. And it doesn't stop there. Jesus doesn't merely acknowledge my human nature; he rescues me from it.

Douglas, 39, schoolteacher and dad
Ephesians 6:10–20

These verses have always appealed to me. They remind me that being a Christian is not always a walk in the park. God gives us armour to wear because we sometimes come under attack. I don't want to push the whole warfare concept, but sometimes we need to defend ourselves – spiritually – and sometimes we need to attack – spiritually. God's Word is a sharp sword that cuts through all sorts of nonsense. And his breastplate protects us when we are tempted to do or think the wrong thing. And I like it that Paul tells us to pray all the time.

Ellen, 9, professional kid
Daniel 3

I like this chapter from the Old Testament. I like it because it's about three men who stood up to a king who wanted them to do something they knew was wrong. Everyone was against them, but they were very brave. They stood up for themselves and for God, and that is really good. It must have been very hard, but they did it.

Em, 13, high school student
Luke 19:1–10

A man named Zacchaeus was quite rich and important, but he was unpopular because he was a tax collector for the Romans. He was short, so he climbed a tree to get a glimpse of Jesus when he travelled through Jericho. Jesus sees him, and I think it's great the way Jesus decides to stay at Zacchaeus's house, even though he was disliked by everyone. It shows that Jesus didn't follow what everyone else thought. He had his own ideas. I like the fact that Zacchaeus had a total change of heart and declared a change in his ways. If Zacchaeus can be saved by Jesus, I know that I can too.

Emma, 17, student

1 Corinthians 6:19

This verse about the Holy Spirit encourages me to really think about the way I treat my body, the actions I take and what tremendous gifts God has given us. It reminds me that we have God living in us and that we should be ambassadors, filling our lives with his Word. We must set a good example because there are onlookers watching and judging all the time.

Farls, 40s, proprietor of a CD and DVD shop

Matthew 7:12

The Bible is full of useful advice. Because we have two children, we're concentrating on this particularly relevant and helpful bit of advice quite a bit at the moment.

Geoff, 55, cabinetmaker and builder

Ecclesiastes

I'm a pretty straightforward bloke, and I don't go for too much airy-fairy stuff. The book of Ecclesiastes tells it as it is. The book is real and relevant and applicable. God is in control. Get right with the Lord. God is where you find true meaning in life. All that other stuff of life doesn't really matter very much.

Jane, 34, solicitor

Psalms

I particularly love to read Psalms. This book unequivocally promises us God's faithfulness and strength in times of trouble. It reflects a searching and longing for righteousness before God in our lives. It portrays a majestic Creator who is at the same time a very personal and caring God, and it contains some of the most heart-lifting worship and praise to be found in the Bible.

Liz, 11, student

Genesis 37–50

These chapters tell about the life of an amazing man who faced a lot of hardship. His name was Joseph. He got taken from his family and ended up in another country. But God looked after him and blessed him and had a plan for him. I like it that after many years, he got back with his family again. His life was a big adventure.

Marc, 44, manager, sinner, parent, bloke

The entire Bible

It is amazing, having avoided reading the book most forced down my throat, that I now refer to it regularly. No matter what page you open, there is something to ponder or ease our pain. The instructions are simple. Old ones or new ones, they all make sense and refer to the one essential message of a salvation that is offered for free with no hidden costs. The whole thing adds up. Read it and refer to the instructions.

Mary, my age is none of your business, grandmother and retired secretary

The Gospels

Jesus is my Saviour and my Lord, and I love to read about him. There are the accounts of his amazing birth, all of his teachings and miracles and of course his death and resurrection. The most powerful words in the Bible to me are those of John 3:16. They tell us that God sent his Son Jesus into the world to die and to give eternal life. This is the main message of the Bible. Jesus is the Saviour. Amen!

MJ, 35, banker and mother

Mark 4

The teachings of Jesus are particularly powerful. He sometimes spoke by telling parables, which were stories with hidden meanings. The parable of the sower is the story of the different reactions that people have to God's Word. As a Christian, I have seen this parable come true in a number of different people I have known. Jesus taught and spoke with a cutting sense of truth, and his words are equally as meaningful today as they were back then.

Max, 15, student

Judges 15 and 16

I like reading this book because the judges were amazing people and leaders. They lived in a very violent time, and they had to be tough. Samson in chapters 15 and 16 was a violent guy and a bit crazy, I think. I like the way he prayed to God and as a final act got revenge on the people who had tortured him.

Nathan, 23, Uni student and aspiring lawyer

Matthew 16, particularly verses 25 and 26

I love it when Jesus cuts through our wondering about him and makes his plan clear. I find Peter's earnest confession of Jesus' identity touching, and I am compelled by Jesus' call to get a little bit reckless and rely on him in order to know God.

Dr Nerida, 28, animal scientist and mother

1 Peter 2:9

The Bible contains answers to life's big questions, and its message gives our daily life significance and purpose. In a world where science can explain the complex intricacies of the mechanics of our existence, we can sometimes feel very insignificant. In a world where we are bombarded with messages that tell us we must achieve X, own Y and look like Z in order to be a success, the Bible tells us why we really exist and who we are in this vast universe.

Reuben, 30, account manager and father of a small dynasty

Philippians 4:13

I like this verse because I know that in my own strength I will never get to where I want to go in life. The Bible teaches us to be bigger people than we would ordinarily be – to stretch ourselves beyond our capabilities. But God doesn't expect us to do it by ourselves. He gave us Jesus Christ to get us there. This verse sums up that sentiment beautifully. It reminds me that Christ strengthens me.

Richard, 40+, computer technician

Proverbs 3:5–8

This has been my favourite passage for many years. Proverbs is a book full of helpful advice. Think about the implications of these verses, and if you make this your guiding principle in life, you will never go wrong.

Dr Rod, 37, research scientist

Romans 1:20

In the Bible I see a God who is consistent, mysterious, relational and who uses themes. In creation I see these same characteristics: from the mystery of quantum mechanics to the theme of the genetic code that is shared by all living things. The fact that we can do science at all relies on the assumption that the laws of the universe are consistent through space-time. Finally, I see a creation that is profoundly relational, with each component summing together to make the many and varied things we find in our universe.

Ruth, 43, artist and mother

Acts

Acts is such an exciting book, telling of one of the most important periods of history. Jesus has gone and his band of followers head off, empowered by the Holy Spirit, into the world to tell everyone about Jesus. I enjoy reading of their amazing adventures as they travel and meet all sorts of different people. They perform miracles and are chased out of towns. They survive a riot, storms and shipwrecks. Some are arrested and imprisoned. All the while, they preach and spread the good news about Jesus. It would make a great movie!

Simon, 35, software engineer, husband and dad

Galatians 6:11

Christians have a habit of writing meaningful verses on birthday cards. I always write this verse reference on cards in really big letters as a joke. There's plenty of good serious stuff in the Bible. But this verse amuses me.

Tsung, 14, student

Galatians 5:22–23

I have these verses written on a card in my wallet. They remind how God's Holy Spirit controls my life and how I should be living my life as a Christian.

Victoria, 27, student

The whole Bible!

I like the Bible because it lets me know who God is. It is God's way of communicating with us. I like to be reminded of his promises and that he is true, always, to his Word. I love that it encourages me to be Christlike, and how to do that, and that it has great passages for when I feel up and great passages for when I feel down. It is amazing they were written so long ago! Someone felt just like I do, that long ago? It is inspiring. Which part do I like the best? I'm afraid I can't single out just one part. The whole thing!

William, 58, semiretired mechanic

Jonah

People often think of the prophets as being very formal and holy people. I like reading about Jonah because he was very human in all he thought and did. He tried running away from God and didn't want to do what God wanted him to do. He got grumpy and angry and self-righteous. I can relate to him as being someone who is flawed, and I like the fact that the Bible has real people in it. They are not always perfect individuals that I can't relate to.

The message of the Bible is constant and unchanging. But we all have verses or passages or parts of the Bible that, for whatever reason, are particularly important, memorable or significant to us. You have just read what a bunch of people think about various bits of the Bible. But they haven't even scratched the surface of the Bible's depths. There are so many more people and events and teachings to discover.

It's interesting to read what other people have encountered in the Bible. It can introduce us to people and places and ideas we might not normally come across by ourselves. We'd be interested to hear about your experiences, readings, and reactions to the Bible too. What does the Bible mean to you? What are your favourite sections? How does it impact your life?

So we want to invite you to contribute your own comments to our **Internet blog.** Simply go to **www.everythingaboutthebible.com** and add your entry. We'd be really interested to read what you have to say.

We'd also love to hear what you think about our book . . . as long as it's complimentary! Rocket science and a degree in English literature not prerequisite.

Well folks, that about does it. This book has come to an end. But now it's time for the good stuff. Go and read the Bible for yourself. Let the adventure begin.

Ben and Pete

Hey Pete, where did all the words go?　　　　　　—Ben

It's the end, Ben. The book is finished.　　　　　　—Pete

Alright! You mean we get our weekends back now?　　—Ben

Yep. But I have an idea for another book.　　　　　—Pete

Ben?　　　　　　　　　　　　　　　　　　　　　—Pete

Ben?　　　　　　　　　　　　　　　　　　　　　—Pete

I'm sorry. Ben's not available right now. Please leave a
message at the prompt.　　　　　　　　　　　　—Ben

We want to hear from you. Please send your comments about this
book to us in care of zreview@zondervan.com. Thank you.

GRAND RAPIDS, MICHIGAN 49530 USA
WWW.ZONDERVAN.COM